Superheroes and Masculinity

Superheroes and Masculinity

Unmasking the Gender Performance of Heroism

Edited by
Sean Parson and J. L. Schatz

LEXINGTON BOOKS
Lanham • Boulder • New York • London

Published by Lexington Books
An imprint of The Rowman & Littlefield Publishing Group, Inc.
4501 Forbes Boulevard, Suite 200, Lanham, Maryland 20706
www.rowman.com

6 Tinworth Street, London SE11 5AL

British Library Cataloguing in Publication Information Available

Library of Congress Control Number: 2019915048

ISBN 978-1-4985-9149-2 (cloth : alk. paper)
ISBN 978-1-4985-9150-8 (electronic)

♾™ The paper used in this publication meets the minimum requirements of American National Standard for Information Sciences Permanence of Paper for Printed Library Materials, ANSI/NISO Z39.48-1992.

Contents

Introduction

The Purpose and Intent of Our Project

This collection of chapters looks to forms of masculinity—both restorative and toxic—within the superhero genre to explore how gender operates in our society and to critically untangle how forms of masculinity are reproduced. This timely intervention is necessary given the increased primacy of super-heroes on the media marketplace. Superhero films have shattered box office numbers (Perry 2019). They have also thrived on both streaming services like Netflix as well as on cable television networks (Alexander 2017). As a result, more people are seeing their identities and beliefs influenced by the way that superheroes are represented. In turn these stories are actively shap-ing our national identities.

For a country like the United States that has been at war for eighteen consecutive years these national identities are often centered around hege-monic masculinity. No doubt,

> male-centric production and consumption of comic books results in a hyper-masculine character presentation of male characters and a hyper-fetishized and hypersexualized presentation of female characters. In addition, these character types have become more exaggerated during the seven decades that this study analyzes. The result is that the most hyperbolic bodies for male and female characters appear in contemporary comics. Furthermore, [. . .] it is essential to move beyond gendered obsession to create a comic book superhero that better represents realistic, human-embodied achievements and combats the dangers of body obsession present in contemporary American society. (Avery-Natale 2013, 72–73)

1

In many ways superheroes reinforce hegemonic masculinity, promoting a conception that centralizes violence, power, and control. Fortunately, beyond the hegemonic formations of masculinity there are alternative understandings that can also be read into how superheroes operate. In short, "men who reject part or all of orthodox masculinity must construct and defend alternative gender identities[. Ultimately, . . .] non-hegemonic masculinities may undermine hegemonic masculinity by rejecting certain elements of hegemonic masculinity while maintaining others" (De Visser, Smith, and McDonnell 2009, 1056). The complex knot of masculinity, which has received increasing focus in mainstream media, is difficult to untangle and the conversation often illicits intense reactions. This collection hopes to circumvent this intense reaction, while pulling free important strands within the knot before us, by focusing on cultural representations. These representations both mirror and shape reality. As such, looking to them provides both insight into how masculinity operates and also provides critical counter-hegemonic discourses that can be used to channel energy toward liberation. This collection ultimately aims at exploring how the intersection of masculinity and superheroes operate, thereby informing the gendered expectations forged out of what it means to be a hero in the first place.

Further as media representations about what it means to be a hero, is informed by (hetero)national narratives, unpacking how these narratives operate is necessary in understanding the consequences of the patriarchal imaginations. As Cynthia Weber (1999) demonstrates, "when putting on America's imaginary body, Americans blend into the supposedly colorless corporeality of the United States—whiteness, a hegemonic hue that is 'everything and nothing[.' . . .] Read through that supposition, this American body is [. . .] not just any caped crusader but a man in a dress[, . . .] marked by both the presence of the phallus [. . .] and the absence of the phallus" (6). While Weber (1999) doesn't write in relation to superheroes her work on how political cartoons informed the public discourse about international events is telling, given how often the supervillain has been represented by Hollywood as being an enemy to the United States—and therefore the entire planet. Whether it be the Nazis with the Red Skull in *Captain America: The First Avenger* (2011), *Wonder Woman* (2017), or *Hellboy* (2004), or global terrorist syndicates as in *Iron Man 3* (2013) or *Batman Begins* (2005)—the threat is always existential and the status quo must be protected and maintained by a hero, who in defending the United States defends the world. Naturally, none of these examples are without their historic media precursors, whether it be in the form of the *Indiana Jones* saga, *Air Force One* (1997), *Independence Day* (1996), the political cartoons Weber writes about, or any number of old Westerns and anti-Soviet films throughout history of American media. All told, investigating how superheroes operate is imperative for understanding how the contemporary imperial form of hegemony both develops and sustains itself in spite of the violence that it creates in the name of peace.

To this end, Jasbir Puar (2007) contends that the

> deployment of exception and exceptionalism works to turn the negative valence of torture into the positive register of the valorization of (American) life, that is, torture in the name of the maximization and optimization of life. As the U.S. nation-state produces narratives of exception through the war on terror, [. . . its] discourse functions through transnational displacements that suture spaces of cultural citizenship in the United States for homosexual subjects as they concurrently secure nationalist interests globally. In some instances these narratives are explicit, as in the aftermath of the release of the Abu Ghraib photos, where the claims to exceptionalism resonated on many planes for U.S. citizen-subjects: morally, sexually, culturally, "patriotically." This imbrication of American exceptionalism is increasingly marked through or aided by certain homosexual bodies, which is to say, through homonationalism. (3–5)

In other words, the imperial projects put forth in the name of homonationalism come at the direct cost of lives that don't fit within the normative construction of what it means to be a "good" (male/female, masculine/feminine) citizen. This false binary construction of identity often distorts queer interpretations and places them back within heteronormative constructs, as is commonly seen in the gay marriage political debate. Ultimately, while gender, sexuality, and sex have tenuous relationships to biology, states continue to use arbitrary markers as a basis for policy in ways that insidiously target those who don't fit within these definitions. As this becomes graphed onto things like citizenship it enables policies of imprisonment, internment, mass exportations, and supposedly reasonable calculations of collateral damage (i.e., civilian deaths). No doubt, "the factioning, fractioning, and fractalizing of identity is a prime activity of societies of control, whereby subjects (the ethnic, the homonormative) orient themselves as subjects through their disassociation or disidentification from others disenfranchised in similar ways in favor of consolidation with axes of privilege" (Puar 2007, 28). To work against this violence requires both direct action against its most explicit manifestations and also continually challenge the normative stories that allow such violence to be understood as heroic in the first place.

When these homonationalist narratives become normalized through media representations, it is suddenly evident the link between people joining the Army and the U.S. military spending over one billion dollars per year in advertising, including screened ads before the blockbuster hits the theater (Footerman 2018). In short, it is not by accident that "superheroes such as Captain America came to be lasting symbols of patriotic American values," even if he might sometimes fight against certain elements of government (Mercier 2008, 28).

> In fact, the question of what a superhero is has become central to our culture's
> understanding of itself and our future. The superhero genre has [. . .] served as
> a useful metaphorical way of discussing immigration, Americanization, urban-
> ization, American identity, changing conceptions of race and gender, individu-
> alism, capitalism, modernism, and so many other central cultural concerns.
> (Rosenberg and Coogan 2013, xvii–xviii)

Sadly, so often media—and superheroes in particular—are written off as just entertainment, and the opportunity to scrutinize the media ties to corporate and military funding as well as the dissecting of the larger ideological, and gendered structures within the medium goes missing. Even in those few places where comics studies is given attention within the academy, those educational institutions and journals have had a tendency to favor more "seri-ous-minded" graphic novels while passing over the genre of superheroes (Hatfield, Heer, and Worcester 2013, xi). While this work on graphic novels as well as postcolonial and queer studies are not without their merit, attention to how superheroes function in the cultural imagination is an important nexus point for understanding the beacons of truth and justice they are often called upon to represent.

Fortunately, where there is power there is resistance, and by continuing to tear small holes in the hegemonic screen it may be possible to alter the representations surrounding heroism and masculinity for the better. At the very least it would help challenge the discursive ideological foundation for the current homonationalist enterprise and toxic masculinity of the United States. No doubt, some of this work is being done already, exploring a diversity of important topics from race (Nama 2011; Gateward and Jennings 2015; Howard and Jackson 2013) to disability (Alaniz 2014; Foss, Gray, and Whalen 2016), and critical animal studies (Schatz and Parson 2017). In fact, there has even been some increasingly insightful work done on queerness (Fawaz 2016) and gender (Cocca 2016; Gray and Kaklamanidou 2011; Ma-drid 2016) in relation to graphic novels and comics. This collection seeks to expand upon this work by understanding how masculinity in particular par-ticipates in the reproduction of patriarchal understandings of heroism, and where alternative configurations of what it means to be masculine can be forged outside heteronormative binaries. To do so, the chapters included in this book seek not only to unpack negative representations of hypermasculin-ity in superhero films and comics, or even just the toxic Geek culture that targets women beyond these representations, they also look toward critical readings that can craft new ways of understanding and approaching super-heroes that can queer the normalizing narratives that serve as the foundation to homonationalist violence. Taken together this collection serves to offer both a critique of prevailing heteronormative and patriarchal representations as well as a means to sketch alternatives to provide the seeds of resistance.

While some may still claim that there is more important work to be done challenging the literal practices of mass incarceration, genocide, the threat of environmental apocalypse, racial injustice, and patriarchal violence, we believe that this work on superheroes—and critical cultural studies more generally—is every bit as crucial in challenging those practices. As Judith Butler (1988) effectively argues,

> The tacit collective agreement to perform, produce, and sustain discrete and polar genders as cultural fictions is obscured by the credibility of its own production. The authors of gender become entranced by their own fictions whereby the construction compels one's belief in its necessity and naturalness. The historical possibilities materialized through various corporeal styles are nothing other than those punitively regulated cultural fictions that are alternately embodied and disguised under duress. (522)

As a result, it is imperative to interrogate the discursive underpinnings of superheroes as a reference point because they help to normalize the very violence done in the name of being a hero, protecting America, enforcing justice, and saving the world. Without these rhetorical webs to reproduce the way people learn about binary constructions of identity (men/women, good/evil, and so on) the very scaffoldings that underpin the more literal instantiations of violence will come undone. Again, none of this is to say that the work of direct action against policies of internment, indiscriminate warfare, and judicialized violence is unimportant. It is instead highlighting the ways in which economics, violence, and culture are interconnected and mutually reinforcing. In short, it is to contend that sacrificing superheroes as an avenue of analysis to how those policies operate, and are understood in the minds of citizens who believe such policies are necessary for the greater good, forfeits a crucial node of resistance given the nationalist furor surrounding superheroes today. At the very least, our approach does not trade off with other actions and analysis against oppression. At the best, it adds another crucial front in the necessary battle against hegemonic masculinity since its presence exists both in the real world and the cultural imaginary in which it's envisioned. So long as these two venues for opposition remain disconnected it will be very difficult to do anything besides continually play catch up and apply Band-Aids to the collateral damage done by patriarchal policymaking.

This tie between media and gendered identity has been proven as study after study illustrates how movies, television, and advertising likely influences a person's sense of self, even if unconsciously (Gauntlett 2002; Kellner 1995; Thornham 1999). The box office dominance of superheroes, the litany of television shows, and the continual sales of superhero comic books demonstrates a clear venue for analysis because of the passive, and uncritical ways, in which superheroes seep into our collective and individual unconscious. This could not be any more apparent than when there's an ad for the

Marines before a preview of *Lone Survivor* (2013) or before the screening of *Thor: The Dark World* (2013), each featuring a white hypermasculinized male protagonist saving the day—next to his supporting cast of women and minorities. The fact advertisers, moviemakers, and theaters continually make these connections is because they continue to work, selling more tickets than ever and continually recruiting more Marines. Consuming this media uncritically enables those profits at the box office to translate into cultural capital that continues to buy the mindsets of the people, enabling them to sit idly by as their neighbors are deported, shot, or locked away. By critically investigating these narratives, and understanding how they become tied to manhood and nationhood, we can help resist and ensure other representational possibilities exist. This collection seeks to do precisely that.

OVERVIEW OF BOOK AND CHAPTER OUTLINE

To realize the goal of our collection, our book is divided into two sections in order to cohesively develop the need for this intervention, a powerful critique of prevailing representations of hegemonic masculinity, and alternative arrangements of how masculinity can operate. We also hope that this construction helps both the newer and more advanced reader of cultural comics and gender studies to their particular interests. By dividing the book between critique and alternative our hope is to demonstrate how, despite the problematic portrayals that currently exist, that different representations are out there ready to be read. Thus, our hope is to move from an indictment of the superhero genre at large to a sense of optimism and hope that the hegemonic gender representations can indeed change for the better.

We begin our book by exploring how masculinity is constructed in superhero narratives in order to help give the reader a better avenue for understanding how these norms can be reconstructed. Together these chapters explore different configurations of gender from toxic masculinity to bromance, as well as the material consequences for those who fall outside the hegemonic norms. This foundation for the book is essential since it not only helps establish a common vocabulary for the reader but also frames the problems the second section will take up and provide alternatives to. At the same time, the range of individual comics and superheroes in this section will hopefully be appealing to a wide array of readers because of the diversity of narratives that are taken up. In short, this section provides the theoretical tools for readers to better understand how to deconstruct and explore masculinity within the superhero genre as a whole.

The first chapter of our collection by Anne Bialowas and Ryan Cheek explores the way bromances operate in superhero franchises in order to provide heterosexual coverage for what otherwise might be understood as homosocial bonding between male superheroes and their sidekicks. In this chapter the reader will discover the strategies deployed by superheroes in order to consolidate their hegemonic masculine primacy vis-à-vis their sidekicks in order to ensure their readers and viewers that, while they might love their male partners in fighting crime, they are still decidedly heterosexual and a real man's man. These strategies deployed by directors, artists, and writers ultimately distort moments of nonnormative gender expression back into an otherwise heteronormative genre in order to remain marketable to the masses.

Chapter 2 by Hailey J. Austin takes a look at how the creation of the female Thor in one of Thor's later iterations was ultimately hijacked by a toxic fan base in order to perpetuate patriarchal understandings of the hero, and its creators. Austin points out that, while there was the possibility for a message of feminist empowerment in the female Thor, this narrative got downplayed within both the story arc and the way its narrative circulated around social media. By paying attention to how bloggers responded, and then subsequently harassed Marvel's editorial and creative staff, Austin demonstrates how the comics industry was ultimately willing to succumb to the pressure and strip Thor of her female mantle and return it back to a man, thereby reassuring the heteronormative nature of the God of Thunder.

Kevin Cummings, in the third chapter of this collection, explores how *Marvel 1602* portrays the age of superheroes in the time of witch hunts and how the demonization of difference in the comics parallels that which happened in reality. He ultimately goes on to demonstrate that the patriarchal belief structures, encouraged and supported by the development of capitalism, was used to target women who stepped out of their more traditional roles in the home and started to achieve economic independence for themselves. Like in reality, the mutants in *Marvel 1602* also faced persecution for being different and seeking to live their lives outside of the traditional values society was forcing upon others. Ultimately, this chapter makes the connection between how close reality and the comics really are.

In chapter 4, Jacob Murel explores how the Joker in *The Dark Knight* (2008) is poised as a queer villain that threatens not just the citizens of Gotham City but also the gendered expectations of society at large. In doing so, Murel demonstrates how queerness is inherently poised as threatening to the dominant heteronormative order and the nation-state system in general. By building upon Puar's theories of homonationalism, he shows how the most threatening acts come about not just through physical violence but through terrorist assemblages waged on the symbolic order that maintains the neat binary boundaries between male/female, masculine/feminine, hetero/homosexual, and so on.

After these first four chapters, the second section of our book moves away from a critique of the superhero genre in order to explore alternative constructions of masculinity and gender. The goal for this section is to end the book on an optimistic note and provide some guidance and support for the reader to navigate the world of masculinity, sexuality, and identity. In doing so, this section returns to a wider range of superheroes in order to better understand the nonnormative configurations of masculinity that already exists in the genre. Collectively, the authors of this section demonstrate that not all superheroes need to reify toxic masculinity for their strength and that readers do not always need to look to the margins to reconstruct alternative forms of masculinity. Rather, many superheroes are already fighting to break down patriarchal values and save the world. Ending our book on this note will leave the reader with a sense of the complete superhero genre by pointing them toward new narratives of heroism that can lead us to a better tomorrow.

The section begins with chapter 5 by Julian Barr, David Roberts, and Edgar Sandoval who explore the popular cartoon *Steven Universe*. In it, they demonstrate how there already exists superheroes who don't wield their masculinity as a weapon but rather attempt to reinterpret what it means to be a hero or masculine in the first place. In this way the show's main protagonist, Steven Universe, fashions his heroism through resolving conflict by finding a middle ground with his enemies instead of trying to beat them into submission. At the same time, the show explores how gender can be understood differently and queers the portrayal of masculinity so that it need not always be presented in its hegemonic form. In doing so, they demonstrate a different kind of hero where queerness, not heteronormativity, is the solution to peace throughout the universe.

In chapter 6, Kiera M. Gaswit returns to analyzing the female Thor. Unlike the chapter in the first section of this book, they conclude that Jane Foster's construction as Thor can still be read positively despite the way the story arc ends. For them, the very presentation of a female Thor, without the need to rename the character as Thor Girl, helps to demonstrate how the mantle of heroism can be held by men and women alike without the need to distinguish the gender of the hero because anyone has the power to be super. At the same time, they demonstrate the way Jane Foster portrays Thor is decidedly different than the male version of Thor, and in so doing helps to open space for a female masculinity to be positively expressed and embraced.

T. J. Buttgereit, Emily Mendelson, and J. L. Schatz explore the way Poison Ivy can be read as a model of queer empowerment in chapter 7. In doing so, they both point out how Poison Ivy has been traditionally displayed as lacking agency through her hypersexualized portrayal designed for male consumption, and how we can read against the grain of that interpretation in order to demonstrate the empowerment Poison Ivy has as she steps into the lead of her own story arc. Ultimately, they contend that Poison Ivy exists as a bastion of queer empowerment that stands in stark contrast to many of the other supervillains heroes are put up against to fight. In short, her advocacy for the environment and her means of achieving it help to break down the heteronormative constructions that separate good from bad, male from female, and straight from queer. As such, this chapter seeks to provide the reader with tools to provide counterreadings in order to demonstrate that resistance to the heteronormative order can exist even in those places and characters that are supposedly constructed by men for male consumption.

In chapter 8, Brian Johnson provides a semiautobiographical account of how *The New Teen Titans* helped provide an outlet for nonnormative boys, and girls, to understand what it means to be a hero through the alternative performances of gender the comics displayed. By accounting for how the comics shifted its narrative away from just fighting villains to the everyday life of living as a hero, Johnson contends that this drama-inspired comic book run helped to provide a forum for young readers to move away from the hegemonic depictions of masculinity as always being on the side of good. Instead he contends that *The New Teen Titans* helped to move the comic book industry toward deeper storytelling and character development that championed queer relationships and the ability for even the toughest of men to cry.

Taken as a whole our hope is that this collection will provide the reader with meaningful ways to confront the image of the superhero and unmask the genre's overreliance on the tired tropes of hegemonic masculinity and heteronormativity. Our belief is that through this analysis we can better understand how concepts like nationhood and gender have become interconnected in ways that have provided a metanarrative to support imperial campaigns and wars abroad. Through challenging these narratives, and by exploring alternatives, we believe that it can be possible to undermine the ideological and discursive foundations that allow America's homonationalism to inflict so much violence around the world. By deconstructing the cultural foundations upon which heroism rests provides a path forward to challenge the prevailing heteronormative assumptions that shapes our world, and which seeks to destroy anything that doesn't conform to its logic. From there it can be possible to craft a new politics of imagination where being a hero doesn't mean killing or assimilating those who appear threatening to the dominant order. Ultimately, moving away from such threat construction is essential in order to truly provide peace and justice for all.

REFERENCES

Alaniz, José. 2014. *Death, Disability, and the Superhero: The Silver Age and Beyond*. Jackson: University Press of Mississippi.

Alexander, Julia. 2017. " The CW Is Using Netflix's Formula to Dominate the Superhero Genre on TV." *Polygon*. https://www.polygon.com/2017/1/9/14215208/cw-netflix-flash-ar-row-supergirl.

Avery-Natale, Edward. 2013. "An Analysis of Embodiment among Six Superheroes in DC Comics." *Social Thought and Research* 32: 71–106.

Butler, Judith. 1988. " Performative Acts and Gender Constitution: An Essay in Phenomenology and Feminist Theory." *Theater Journal* 40(4): 519–31.

Cocca, Carolyn. 2016. *Superwomen: Gender, Power, and Representation*. New York: Bloomsbury Academic, an imprint of Bloomsbury Publishing Inc.

De Visser, Richard, Jonathan Smith, and Elizabeth McDonnell. 2009. "'That's Not Masculine: Masculine Capital and Health-Related Behaviour." *Journal of Health Psychology* 14(7): 1047–58.

Fawaz, Ramzi. 2016. *The New Mutants: Superheroes and the Radical Imagination of American Comics*. Postmillennial Pop. New York; London: New York University Press.

Footerman, Mark. 2018. "Pigskins & Propaganda: DoD Recruiting Efforts Costing Taxpayers Millions." *Pursuit*. https://www.ourpursuit.com/pigskins-propaganda-dod-recruiting-ef-forts-costing-taxpayers-millions/.

Foss, Chris, Jonathan W. Gray, and Zach Whalen, eds. 2016. *Disability in Comic Books and Graphic Narratives*. New York: Palgrave Macmillan.

Gateward, Frances K., and John Jennings, eds. 2015. *The Blacker the Ink: Constructions of Black Identity in Comics and Sequential Art*. New Brunswick, NJ: Rutgers University Press.

Gauntlett, David. 2002. *Media, Gender and Identity: An Introduction*. New York: Routledge.

Gray, Richard J., and Betty Kaklamanidou, eds. 2011. *The 21st Century Superhero: Essays on Gender, Genre and Globalization in Film*. Jefferson, NC: McFarland.

Hatfield, Charles, Jeet Heer, and Kent Worcester. 2013. *The Superhero Reader*. Jackson, MS: University Press of Mississippi.

Howard, Sheena C., and Ronald L. Jackson, eds. 2013. *Black Comics: Politics of Race and Representation*. London; New York: Bloomsbury Academic.

Kellner, Douglas. 1995. *Cultural Studies, Identity and Politics Between the Modern and the Postmodern*. New York: Routledge.

Madrid, Mike. 2016. *The Supergirls: Fashion, Feminism, Fantasy, and the History of Comic Book Heroines*. Revised and Updated edition. Ashland, OR: Exterminating Angel Press.

Mercier, Sebastian. 2008. "'Truth Justice and the American Way:' The Intersection of American Youth Culture and Superhero Narratives." *Iowa Historical Review* 1(2): 21–59. http://ir.uiowa.edu/cgi/viewcontent.cgi?article=1010&context=iowa-historical-review.

Nama, Adilifu. 2011. *Super Black: American Pop Culture and Black Superheroes*. 1st ed. Austin: University of Texas Press.

Perry, Spencer. 2019. "The Highest Grossing Superhero Movies of All-Time." *Superhero Hype*. https://www.superherohype.com/features/372133-the-highest-grossing-superhero-movies-of-all-time.

Puar, Jasbir K. 2007. *Terrorist Assemblages: Homonationalism in Queer Times*. Durham: Duke University Press.

Rosenberg, Robin, and Peter Coogan. 2013. *What Is a Superhero?* Oxford, UK: Oxford University Press.

Schatz, J. L., and Sean Parson, eds. 2018. *Superheroes and Critical Animal Studies: The Heroic Beasts of Total Liberation*. Lanham, Maryland: Lexington Books.

Thornham, Sue. 1999. *Feminist Film Theory: A Reader*. Edinburgh, UK: Edinburgh University Press.

Trumbore, Dave. 2017. "Superhero Cinemath: Who Won the Battle of the Box Office in 2016?" The Collider. http://collider.com/superhero-movies-box-office-winner-2016/#best-opening-weekend.

Weber, Cynthia. 1999. *Faking It: US Hegemony in a "Post-Phallic" Era*. Minneapolis, MN: University of Minnesota Press.

Chapter One

Deconstructing the Hero-Sidekick Bromance

Foggy, Kato, and the Masculine Performance of Friendship

Anne Bialowas and Ryan Cheek

Sidekicks are a common feature of the superhero media genre. As junior partners, sidekicks are narrative foils for the hero protagonist (e.g., as comic relief, straight-person, mentees, sex appeal, and/or confidants). Friendship is a gendered performance that operationalizes social norms for both same-gender and opposite-gender relationships (Flannery and Smith 2017, 617). Sidekicks that are coded as masculine and have a close friendship with a masculine superhero offer a unique opportunity to analyze the masculine performance of friendship. This chapter interrogates the relationships that the sidekick characters Foggy and Kato have with their respective superhero counterparts, Daredevil and the Green Hornet. The analysis will focus on the 20th Century Fox film *Daredevil* (2003), the Netflix television adaptation *Daredevil* (2015), the ABC television series *The Green Hornet* (1966), and the Columbia Pictures film *The Green Hornet* (2011). This chapter takes a critical feminist rhetorical perspective to highlight five bromance strategies employed in these narratives to heteronormatively straighten same-sex male friendships in order to make them safe for mass consumption.

A critical feminist rhetorical perspective is interested in the analysis of gender in a rhetorical artifact. It then evaluates the use of rhetoric to define women and men and/or femininity and masculinity while discovering ways in which certain values, practices, and performances are gendered, privileged, and/or marginalized. Thus, a feminist approach more grounded in critical assumptions explores how "gender, race, discourse, [and] power

13

[. . .] intersect to produce relations of dominance and resistance" while also noting that sometimes critical studies can overlook the role of gender (Ashcraft and Mumby 2004, 49). This does not mean a feminist approach is critical just by "adding" issues of race or class with gender, but rather assuming that gender in itself is not an essential or exclusive unifying term without needing further critical exploration.

Furthermore, this chapter is also informed by an intersectional approach. Using the metaphor of intersectionality as a frame, Collins (2000) describes the interlocking systems of oppression that help pivot the center of analysis, allowing for "new themes, approaches, and questions [to] become visible" (44). Instead of analyzing issues of difference like race, class, gender, and sexuality as separate systems of oppression, Collins (2000) argues that "the construct of intersectionality references how these systems mutually construct one another. Intersectional paradigms suggest that certain ideas and/or practices surface repeatedly across multiple systems of oppression" (47–48). Intersectionality is not a strictly feminist tool but taking a feminist approach does allow for the inclusion of issues of difference with regard to gender, race, class, and sexuality in one's analysis (Crenshaw 1997; Moon and Nakayama 2005; Nakayama 1994). A feminist rhetorical approach is especially complemented by intersectional analysis because a focus on power relations is central to understanding how multiple discourses influence the construction of masculine friendships in superhero texts.

THE BACKSTORY OF BROMANCE

According to Nardi (1992), images of ideal friendships are "often expressed in terms of women's traits: intimacy, trust, caring, and nurturing, thereby excluding the more traditional men from true friendship" (1). This notion of the "ideal" friendship obviously privileges the verbal expression of intimacy, but an exploration into the representation of how men express friendship is connected more broadly in understanding masculinity in society (Wood and Inman 1993, 279). Past television depictions of male and female friendships from 1950–1980 has upheld these gendered assumptions and stereotypes about friendships. In fact, intimate relationships among men were more than likely to be seen in comedies rather than drama or action adventure genres, with many programs depicting males bonding through their shared engagement through physical acts rather than through emotional disclosure (Spangler 1992, 93). Recently, the concept of "bromance" has infiltrated popular culture as it "has come to denote an emotionally intense bond between presumably straight males who demonstrate an openness to intimacy that they neither regard, acknowledge, avow, nor express sexually" (DeAngelis 2014, 1). *The 40-Year-Old Virgin* (2005) is an early example of a film that encapsulates this male friendship and use of the term "bromance." However, instead of seeing "bromance" as a genre in film, we agree with Becker's (2014) theorization of "bromance" as a "cultural discourse—a way to talking and thinking about male friendships that helps to produce specific ways of feeling and experiencing homosocial intimacy and masculinity" (129). Sedgwick (1985) theorized the term homosocial to distinguish it from homosexual to represent a form of male bonding that often carries with it a fear over homosexuality. The discourse of bromance builds upon her classic unpacking of the homosocial-homosexual continuum in which many depictions of male relationships can be rigidly defined (Sedgwick 1985, 17).

Images of male friendships in media have evolved over time with "buddy films," during the 1970s, as a point of reference (Wood 2003, 198). However, the increased visibility of gay sexual identity in the 1990s paired with increased social acceptance of LGBTQ issues in the 2000s "altered cultural constructions of masculinity and male bonding [that . . .] fueled the rise of the bromance discourse" (Becker 2014, 130). Furthermore, these mediated "scenarios forced straight men to establish their heterosexuality—and to find a way to do so without appearing homophobic" (Becker 2014, 132). This is not to say that more gay friendly media representations erased all homophobia. No doubt, homophobia exists "as a well-worn convention serving as a cinematic alibi for straight male homosociality" (Boyle and Berridge 2014, 361). Rather, "when queer culture was widely perceived as impacting popular taste" then mediated expressions of male bonding and friendship was strategically reaffirmed through straight male homosociality in nuanced ways (Feil 2014, 93). Essentially, the term "bromance" in and of itself acts rhetorically in popular discourse to reaffirm the appearance of a straight man being close with another man while not jeopardizing their hegemonic masculinity or identity as straight.

Beyond the rhetorical term "bromance" being used, research has uncovered other strategies and nuanced ways of how media representations of male friendships maintain the appearance of being straight while upholding traditional masculinity. In many instances a male's heterosexual relationship already exists before male friends meet for the first time in most bromance films. This convention allows the romantic relationship to appear solid while also acting as a narrative structuring device of a birth (*Due Date*, for instance) or a wedding (*The Hangover*, as an example). Grounding the narrative in such heteronormative experiences provides "a time frame for the homosocial adventures [and can . . .] assuage any homosexual anxieties from the outset" of the film (Boyle and Berridge 2014, 360). Another strategy is through a type of vulgar gross-out humor that marginalizes and objectifies both female and gay male characters (Feil 2014, 97). There is an additional "gross-out" element with the abuse of the male body in such examples like the *Jackass* series (Feil 2014, 101). Another trend in televised narratives

(*Rescue Me*, for example) is the appearance of physically imposed boundaries against women in "boys' clubs" and the intense bromance relationships in workplace settings. Put simply, "these enclaves allow for uncritical expression of retrograde, sexist attitudes and harassing behaviors" (Nettleton 2016, 574). Within the backdrop of the bromance discourse, these nuanced strategies of narrative conventions, types of humor, and perpetuating workplace patriarchy as commonplace allow for hegemonic masculinity to flourish and appearances of deep meaningful same-sex male friendships to be diminished.

A common theme in the traditional buddy movie with men is that their "friendship exists to help the men achieve a set goal (e.g., defeat a common enemy, avert a disaster of cataclysmic proportions" (Boyle and Berridge 2014, 360). This becomes even more apparent with same sex superhero –sidekick relationships. The images of superheroes in media reveal, according to Coyne, Linder, Rasmussen, Nelson, and Collier (2014), "that they portray strong gender stereotypes for males [. . . as they] are generally portrayed as strong, assertive, aggressive, fast, powerful, leaders, and as portraying a muscular ideal body type" (148). Male same-sex superhero friendships are suited for gender analysis because they are situated in a hypermasculine narrative combined with nuanced strategies of maintaining "safe" heteronormative relationships. Some research has begun to explore this dynamic with investigating the Batman/Robin and Superman/Jimmy Olsen relationship. In fact, according to Shyminsky (2011) the superhero is recognized and "made to seem more potent, masculine, and unassailable—he is straightened— through this contrast with his sexually indeterminate or pathologized sidekick" (298). Furthermore, effeminate sidekicks effectively straighten "the central narrative [. . . while] preserving the superhero as a beacon of heternormativity" (Shyminsky 2011, 298). Sidekick characters fulfill different purposes in the lives and narrative progression of their superhero counterparts. The friendship sidekick archetype presents an interesting case to understand masculine norms in society. While not directly related to superhero films, Boyle and Berridge (2014) have noted a trend with male relationships in films as characterized "by a barely concealed antagonism and competition from the outset, and remains structured by inequality throughout" (363).

We argue that the superhero genre both adapts and adds to previously identified bromance strategies intended to straighten protagonist characters to make them acceptable to homophobic viewers. Preexisting heterosexual relationships are difficult to craft for superheroes who are loners. For those heroes with sidekicks, love triangles between the superhero, sidekick, and a single female character (often playing into damsel-in-distress tropes) are manufactured to reinforce the heterosexual nature of the superhero–sidekick friendship. Combat creates the conditions for male friendships to be physically close while retaining a measure of violence to undermine assumptions of sexual intimacy. Like vulgar humor in bromance comedies, physical combat is a bonding experience for male friendships. Hideouts are the superhero equivalent of male-only spaces and provide geographic privacy for the homosocial superhero–sidekick relationship to hide and progress without interference from women or public judgment (Nettleton 2016, 570).

In addition to these adaptations to identified bromance strategies (preexisting relationships, vulgarity, and enclaves), superhero–sidekick friendships highlight two additional themes that undergird male friendship. First, man toys (machines, automobiles, or other gadgets) are excuses for homosocial bonding. In turn, superheroes and their sidekicks invest affections into the technological gadgetry of their trade. The object orientation of their fondness relieves heteroanxiety because of its familiarity to male audience members who routinely bond over cars, guns, and other supposedly manly toys. Second, existential threats posed by antagonists in superhero media create a more concerning villainy for the audience than queerness. In short, characters are straightened by their association with fighting for truth and justice. Close associations between heroes and sidekicks are reframed by a "brothers in arms" trope that transforms homosocial friendship into a more acceptable familial intimacy.

BROMANCING WITH FOGGY AND KATO

Foggy Nelson is the law partner of Matt Murdock, otherwise known as Daredevil. Their relationship has been explored in multiple mediums, including comic books, television, and film. As a friend and colleague of Matt's, who in many characterizations is unaware of his best friend's nighttime vigilante activities, Foggy narratively provides a conscience and comic relief to the seriousness of Daredevil's unwavering commitment to justice. Although he never suits up with Matt, Foggy is every bit his equal in their law practice and often they are friendly rivals competing for a common love interest. Kato is the mononymous name and ambiguously Asian (first depicted as Japanese in the radio program, then Korean or Filipino in early cinema, and most recently Chinese in television and film) driver, mechanic, and sidekick of Britt Reid (the Green Hornet). Superficially, Kato's employment as Britt's driver appears to diminish the argument that he is Britt's equal. However, Kato's martial arts and technological prowess exceed that of his superhero partner in many iterations of their story. In fact, after the television series *The Green Hornet* (1967) floundered after one season in the United States, the show was successfully repackaged and marketed in Asia as *The Kato Show* (Ellis 2015).

Many sidekicks are not equals, either in costume or power abilities, and thus by this very inequitable nature the lawyers Matt Murdock and Foggy

Nelson present an interesting case because they "are not without their own sexual ambiguities and sources of queer anxiety, even if they have gone unnoticed by critics" (Shyminsky 2011, 295). In many ways, Foggy is Matt's foil. Whereas Matt is muscular, masculine, and has superhuman abilities, Foggy is pudgy, effeminate, and merely human. However, they also exhibit many equitable qualities in their skills as lawyers and in their rhetorical abilities, as well as have a tight bond between them because of their shared past. They may fight and yell at one another, but they also support and care for each other as best friends and partners.

We cannot ignore within this analysis the pervasive queer readings that are attached to superhero narratives (Drushel 2014, 257). Nor can we ignore how bromance discourse opens up a space for queer readings (DeAngelis 2014, 9). A queer reading can be understood as nonheteronormative readings by viewers of any sexual orientation (Doty 1993, 7). Drushel (2014) investigated the queering of the *Green Hornet* television series and found it more so queer by association with "the superhero as queer metaphor and in the homosociality of the lead characters" as compared to *Batman* (267). As a consequence, such shows need to alleviate anxiety over gayness in order to win over mainstream audiences and insulate superhero masculinity.

The first strategy to reduce homophobic anxiety surrounding same-sex male friendships is to ground bromance in the narrative plot of a preexisting heterosexual relationship. Whether that is parenthood (e.g., *Due Date* and *Daddy Day Care*), getting married (*The Hangover* and *I Love You, Man*, for instance), or attempting to get laid (*American Pie* and *Superbad*, as examples), heterosexuality is cemented into the plot of many films that center on male friendship. The superhero genre does not escape this trope. Rather, it adapts to it. Juggling multiple identities and secret abilities can foreclose on the ability of superheroes to have children or get married. Instead of preexisting relationships, love triangles are manufactured in same-sex superhero–sidekick friendships to ensure a heterosexual reading of both characters and a narrative straightening that would otherwise be noticeably absent. Men fighting over women is a classic trope of literature that aids in both a heteronormative understanding of male bonding, while securing a competitive masculine climate between male friends (Gambacorta and Ketelaar 2013, 330). In this framing, women are simultaneously obstacles to male friendship and yet critical correctives to the perceived gayness of male characters.

In the Netflix series *Daredevil*, Karen Page is the object of Matt and Foggy's love triangle. She is usually portrayed as the secretary for the law firm Nelson and Murdock, and often finds herself in precarious positions that require the help from one or both of her employers. Sometimes that means she has been kidnapped and needs Daredevil to fight for her, and other times it means she is in legal jeopardy and needs Foggy's rhetorical skill to get her out of trouble. In the comics, Karen is often the damsel-in-distress. However, she finds a new evolution in the Netflix series. In fact, within the Netflix series, Karen has her own heroic character progression exhibiting increasing investigative independence. Despite this resistance to the damsel-in-distress trope, the Marvel Cinematic Universe version depicts a classic love triangle where Foggy desires Karen even though she is enamored with Matt, who appears to be attracted to Karen but whose attention and affections are split.

Although no one gets what they want out of the triangle, everyone's heterosexuality is reaffirmed by its mere existence. Throughout the series, as well as in other versions of *Daredevil*, various female characters play the object of affection role, including Claire Temple (aka Night Nurse) and Elektra. Although the straightening effect is the same for both the superhero and the sidekick in this arrangement, the means by which that effect occurs is different. As the superhero protagonist, Matt is often desired by the women in the triangle. His one-night stands and brief hookups similarly reaffirm Matt's heterosexuality while underscoring his emotional unavailability to women. In contrast, Foggy's pudgy physique and gentle demeanor betray his heterosexuality and make him an object of friendship rather than desire for women in the triangle. Like a gay best friend, Foggy is someone to be trusted emotionally but kept at a distance from physical intimacy (Firth, Raisborough, and Klein 2010, 474). However, by playing on the sexist trope of the "friend zone," this narrative rejects a queer interpretation of Foggy in favor of a "nice guys finish last" framing, which excuses his romantic failures as a common heteronormative experience for men without superhero bodies and super-mysterious lives (Urbaniak and Kilmann 2003, 414).

Traditionally, *The Green Hornet* (1967) television series and its comic book and radio show predecessors demonstrated similar love triangles that emphasized the unavailable straightness of the male superhero Britt Reid contrasted with the feminized straightness of his male sidekick Kato. In every version of the narrative, Lenore Case is a secretary at the Reid-owned *Daily Sentinel* who is aware of the secret identities of the Green Hornet and Kato. Britt is a wealthy playboy newspaper publisher by day and a debonair antihero vigilante by night, whereas Kato is a working-class martial arts master and technological guru whose ethnic ambiguity plays into racist stereotypes of mysterious Asian characters (as gifted and loyal servants to white protagonists) in detective literature from the same era (Simila 2008, 14).

In *The Green Hornet* (2011) movie, Britt Reid is depicted as a misogynist who sexually harasses Lenore Case, who is more interested in Kato's subtle affections. The protagonist superhero is revealed as a chauvinistic antihero with minimal skills and a lot of privilege while the exotic hard-working genius minority sidekick attracts Lenore until a jealous and overentitled Britt sabotages their relationship. However, this reversal of the straightening process in the superhero–sidekick relationship does not remedy the dependence of the plot on racist stereotypes about Asian identity. Instead, in excusing Britt's behavior, this reversal modernizes and entrenches the heteronormative and white supremacist framings of Britt and Kato's superhero–sidekick bromance. Lenore's preference for Kato challenges Britt's self-assumed socioeconomic and racial superiority. Britt's reactions to Kato's attempt to date Lenore exhibits white male fragility and rage (Anderson 2016, 75; DiAngelo 2018, 55). In fact, their interpersonal conflict escalates to physical, emotional, and economic violence when Britt fires Lenore and Kato as a way to sabotage their relationship. At first, Lenore poses an obstacle for the Britt/Kato dyad to overcome. Once she is let in on their secret identities (thus dissolving the love triangle), she fades into the background as a supporting character to the superhero–sidekick duo.

Ultimately, the love triangle strategy corrects same-sex male friendships by grounding their relationships in heteronormative narratives. Similar to bromantic texts straightened by narrative arcs centered on weddings, children, and adolescent desire, the love triangle is a plot device that insulates superheroes and sidekicks from the perception of queerness. Men fighting (physically, verbally, and proverbially) over the romantic attention of women is another sexist trope of masculine performance. In this context, fighting is an intimate encounter made acceptable for masculinity by its association with violence and its heterosexual teleology.

A second strategy used in comedic bromance films is employing vulgar humor to rhetorically separate male friendship from the polite behavior expected of men in mixed-company settings. Movies such as *Wayne's World* (1992), *Clerks* (1994), and *Dumb and Dumber* (1994) use crude, profane, and sexist language to carve out a discourse that is hostile to women's participation, yet resists queer interpretation. Matt and Foggy do not perceptibly exhibit this strategy, but Britt and Kato make ample use of comedic vulgarity to straighten their friendship. Kato telling Britt "don't be a pussy" or Britt claiming Kato "grew up penis-less on the streets" are just a few examples of vulgar bromance in action. Combined with Britt's sexually harassing comments aimed at Lenore, such as "Kato [. . .] who is the hotty boom botty whose standing right behind me" and "if there is one thing I like on my women, it's balls," masculine vulgarity constructs a discursive space that is hostile to women's participation. This is an intentional strategy made clear by Britt telling his sidekick that "girls are a drag. I'm so glad we have each other Kato," which makes explicit his desire for bromance over romance.

Vulgarity is not just discursive, it also manifests in the physical behavior of the characters. Combat brings Britt and Kato together because their friendship extends into the vigilante realm. Physical closeness is a consequence of combat, not its telos, which makes it a safe form of intimacy for a bromance. Team fighting also requires interdependence between the superhero and sidekick that hints at a deeper level of trust between the two. This same strategy is deployed in the local gym during martial arts classes that convert physical and psychological intimacy into a manly activity through the use of violence. Men can rub up against one another so long as their behavior is contained in a narrative of combat that resists queer connotations (Anderson 2011, 570). Likewise, there is a homoeroticism to male violence in film that is straightened by vulgarity and physical conflict.

Male friendships can be tumultuous and violent. Vulgarity and combat are strategies that play on a broader societal trope of "boys will be boys," which excuses physical and verbalized masculine violence. The heterosexuality of these same-sex superhero–sidekick male friendships is reaffirmed by the relation to violence these men share. A platonic bromance includes vulgarity that is often sexually demeaning toward women. It also includes male bonding over physical violence. The impact of this strategy is a normalization of violent behavior as an innate aspect of male friendship. Whether that violence manifests itself verbally or physically, the ability (and desire) to distance the bromance from queer coding by introducing violent words and deeds is a problematic association for the masculine performance of friendship.

Creating male-only spaces provides narrative cover for intimacy in male friendships. Territorially separated from feminine influences and queer interpretations, men are given clearance to bond in these spaces without being perceived as gay. These masculine enclaves excuse the homosociality of men found in them by naturalizing the absence of women. Genres manifest this strategy in different ways. In *Dead Poets Society* (1989) the enclave is an all-male boarding school. In *The Shawshank Redemption* (1994) the enclave is a maximum security male prison. In *Remember the Titans* (2000) the enclave is the locker room. Although not all superhero narratives deploy this strategy, the ones that do adapt by constructing hideouts because the protagonists in these texts require more privacy and secrecy than students, prisoners, and football players in order to conduct their business, and retreat from public scrutiny.

Hideouts offer superheroes, and occasionally their allies, sanctuary from the dangers of public exposure and evil plots. This is the case for the Green Hornet who has the Hornet's Lair. In *The Green Hornet* (1967) television series only men are depicted in the Hornet's Lair. It is a 1960s man cave complete with living quarters, a study, and a garage where the legendary car "Black Beauty" resides. Aside from Britt and Kato, only their district attorney confidante Frank Scanlon enters the lair for business meetings with the superhero. Lenore Case, another confidante of the crime-fighting duo, is excluded from this male-only space. Although the movie version does not contain explicit references to the Hornet's Lair, Britt's mansion (and in particular the garage where Kato's office is) fulfills all the functions of a secret hideout including housing superhero tech and a hidden entrance/exit. Such exclusive spaces replicate the patriarchal history of male-only clubs. However, they can also be read queerly. Hideouts enable homosocial bonding away from the homophobic judgement of society. It is a queer space where inhibition can be suspended and male intimacy can be reciprocated.

In contrast, *Daredevil* has no such male enclave and does not appear to rely on this bromance strategy. Matt Murdock's customized apartment in the *Daredevil* (2003) movie is a darkly lit brooding place that contains spare suits as well as cane weapons. It is a place he retreats to before and after battles with various antagonists. However, his apartment is not so much a male-only place as it is a Matt-only place. In Netflix's version, his apartment is visited by many different characters at various times, and even the law firm of Nelson and Murdock is routinely occupied by Karen Page, thereby making it a backdrop for the love triangle strategy more than a males-only territory.

As the various Daredevil iterations exemplify, not all superheroes make use of a hideout. And, even for those who do, not all construct them as gendered spaces. For superhero-sidekicks that do rely on the male enclave strategy, the absence of women from these spaces is a feature, not just a consequence, of male bonding. Intimacy is desexualized in this context, making it acceptable for men to drop their guard and become more vulnerable with other men, especially out of view from women. Because male-enclaves are embedded in patriarchal societies, there is a tacit acceptance of their existence as part of male friendship rather than suspected as elements of a queer relationship. In this way, men can share a secret space with one another as an ironic strategy to straighten the perception of their bond.

The contrast between Matt/Foggy and Britt/Kato here deserves some reflection. Matt and Foggy are not a traditional superhero–sidekick relationship in the sense that they do not engage in vigilantism together. Instead, they are best friends and law partners who defend vulnerable people. Britt and Kato do engage in vigilantism together and their shared hideout enables this behavior. Daredevil is a solitary superhero where the Green Hornet is part of a duo, which explains the difference in how hideouts are deployed. However, Daredevil and Foggy still have shared spaces, such as their law firm, where they bond and work together, even if those spaces are not exclusive.

A fourth strategy of bromance can be colloquially expressed as "boys and their toys," an idiomatic term that highlights the sometimes obsessive attachment men have with technology, machines, and gadgetry. This attachment can be transitive for male friendship when men invest their mutual affections into an inanimate object instead of each other. Logically expressed, an example of this might be: male A loves cars, male B loves cars, therefore the friendship between males A and B is a result of their mutual love of cars, not necessarily a love for each other. Mutual attachment to various technologies can be a catalyst for the development of bromance. Technology is culturally coded as a masculine domain and is often "cast in terms of male activities

[. . . as the] tools of work and war" (Wajcman 2010, 144). This, in turn, makes it an acceptable outlet for the expression of straight male affection. Representations of male friendship play on this sociocultural association by foregrounding tech in moments of bonding, which makes vulnerable character moments safe for heteronormative audiences. Proficient control of inanimate tools such as cars, guns, and computers ground male characters and make them attractive to other men while justifying that attraction as platonically distanced by gadgetry.

Superhero narratives are often grounded in technology as well. Some superheroes are only super because of the technology they surround themselves with, rather than some innate supernatural power. Following in the archetype established by Batman, Britt Reid is a wealthy white man with no superhuman abilities. However, his money combined with his friendship with technological guru Kato provides Britt with the tools necessary to become a successful vigilante. Bonding over technology is developed into the bromance between Britt and Kato (who is credited in every iteration of the Green Hornet narrative as the designer of Britt's signature gas gun and iconic militarized vehicle). Exemplifying how these investments in man toys can be discrete, in *The Green Hornet* (2011) movie Britt and Kato's relationship is initiated by Kato's technological solution for making a good cup of coffee.

The man toys strategy sheds light on how men become friends despite their homophobic anxieties. Shared interests in properly masculine technologies become connection points where intimacy can grow. Whether that technology is an iron suit, advanced automobile, or legal brief (in the case of Matt and Foggy) it is heteronormatively acceptable for men to share a mutual love for the tools of their vocation. Queer desire is thus separated from the subjects and invested in the toys they share, making this strategy an advantageous one for male friends anxious about how they are sexually coded. Men who share a love of cars or guns are not read queerly because their mutual love is invested in shared passions, not each other.

The relational phenomenon of "war buddies" describes folks who become friends under the extreme and violent circumstances of warfare. Distinct from the vulgarity and combat strategy, a fifth bromance strategy grounds male friendship in a backstory of battle against an existential evil. For example, *Forrest Gump* (1994), *Saving Private Ryan* (1998), and the HBO miniseries *Band of Brothers* (2001) are all stories about males bonding in battle against communists and Nazis. A bromance borne out of battling a mutual mortal enemy is believable and plays into heteronormative framings of warrior men.

Although not usually a matter of armed conflict on a national scale, same-sex superhero–sidekick male friendships are oriented around fighting evil villains. A supervillain is more than just an antagonist. They are the raison d'etre of the superhero–sidekick existence. Wilson Fisk (Kingpin) is a calculating and shadowy organized crime boss whose elusive identity and master-minded character help to elevate Matt Murdock from petite vigilante to the devil of Hell's Kitchen. Benjamin Chudnofsky (Bloodnofsky) is a comedic caricature of supervillainy whose trademark double barrel desert eagle .45 magnum metaphorically represents his own insecurity over people thinking he is not scary. His quest to expand the territory and control his criminal organization helps to unify Britt and Kato into a more purposeful crime-fighting dynamic duo. A significant part of what makes superheroes super is the exceptionally evil villainy they are destined to fight.

Battling evil is a strategy that distinguishes superhero–sidekick friend-ships from the situational antagonisms of many traditional bromance films such as *Dude, Where's My Car?* (2000) and *Harold and Kumar Go to White Castle* (2004). Facing life-threatening conflict adds depth to characters and gives them a reason to cooperate. This is not just a literary phenomenon; it is a social psychological one as well. The "male warrior hypothesis" postulates that men cooperate better when faced with an intergroup threat (Van Vugt, De Cremer, and Janssen 2007, 19). The Kingpin and Bloodnofsky provide such a threat to the lives of Matt, Foggy, Britt, and Kato. Where situationally developed bromances are shallowly created and superficially depicted through humorously unfortunate events, conflict-driven bromances are thoroughly stress tested in a way that rapidly matures their relationships.

Foggy may not suit up with Daredevil to fight street criminals, but he does offer Matt significant aid in fighting the evil plots of criminal master-minds through the judicial system (and is sometimes even targeted for vio-lence, making him part of the violence narrative). Beyond Kingpin, this lawyerly duo helps protect other heroes from the legal entanglements that result from their vigilante work against the shadowy criminal network known as The Hand. Matt and Foggy build a friendship out of a mutual commitment to fighting forces of injustice even at the risk of encountering violence and death. For a sidekick that does not physically fight with their superhero, Foggy Nelson continuously risks his safety in order to aid his best friend. The embodied evil they battle helps to quickly grow them from young, idealistic new lawyers into despair-resistant male warriors. In contrast, Kato does don a mask and rides with Britt to clean up the city streets. Out of the superhe-ro–sidekick context, a pair of costumed men running around having physical encounters with (mostly) other men may be read queerly. Their care for one another is given a straightened explanation. They are "war buddies" who risk life and liberty to stop indiscriminate killers like Bloodnofsky. *The Green Hornet* (2011) movie demonstrates how the strategy of battling evil villainy turns the juvenile homosociality of a wealthy man-child and his father's mechanic into a pair of mature noir vigilante antiheroes.

Put simply, if you provide men a war to fight, their bonding is sanitized by heteronormative framings of masculinity. Few plot points unify and permit intimacy between men like an evil supervillain does. Existential interdependence on one another excuses behavior that might otherwise be read as queer. The superhero–sidekick closeness is just the inevitable tight bond created when two friends persevere together in the face of adversity. Risking their lives in fight-to-the-death conflicts ostensibly in the service of a higher cause unifies masculine subjects traditionally prone to be competitive, not cooperative, with one another.

THE POST-CREDITS SCENE

Friendships are an important social component for human interactions. Heteronormative society places undue gendered burdens on the types and norms of friendships available to us. Closeness and intimacy are normal qualities of friendship. However, in the context of same-sex masculine friendships, they must also be straightened because of an undercurrent of queer anxiety in a homophobic dominant culture. The relatively recent popular culture trope of bromance plays on homophobic anxiety by discursively carving out a space where men can embody the qualities of romantic relationships with one another while maintaining a straightened perception for others as metaphorical brothers. Such a rhetorical move does not remedy the problematic gender stereotypes and homophobia associated with representations of male friendship in dominant culture. In fact, bromantic discourse often compounds heteronormativity by attempting to straighten queer relationships between men.

By unpacking same-sex male superhero–sidekick relationships in the *Daredevil* productions and *The Green Hornet*, we have revealed five different strategies of bromance that help to perform a heteronormative straightening intended to abate queer anxiety over intimate male friendships. Love triangles help to foreground the heterosexual preferences of superheroes and their sidekicks while playing on sexist tropes that prioritize characterizations of women as sexual objects. Sexually demeaning vulgarity creates discursive spaces that are hostile to women's participation while physical combat enables a form of male closeness unlikely to invoke queer anxiety. Sometimes these spaces become geographically demarcated as male enclaves in superhero hideouts reminiscent of juvenile "boys only" clubhouses. Man toys enable a transitive affection where love and care are exchanged through a mutual fascination and obsession with masculinized crime-fighting technologies. Finally, supervillains provide an exigence for superhero–sidekicks to form tightknit bonds as they risk their lives battling existential evil.

Superheroes are cultural icons that have the potential to inform how we interact with each other and how youth develop a sense of morality at an impressionable time in their development. The same-sex male friendships superhero protagonists form with their sidekicks should be viewed as co-constitutive with dominant heteronormative society. These representations both reflect problematic cultural anxieties over queerness and help to sustain heteronormative understandings of male friendship that truncate authentic male bonding experiences. The impact of the five bromance strategies identified in this chapter help to normalize sexism, homophobia, competition, and violence as natural qualities of male friendship. Hegemonic masculinity is maintained and extended through the straightening of male-male relationships in popular culture texts like *Daredevil* and *The Green Hornet*. It seems then that straight men are not able to be represented in media as developing deep meaningful same-sex relationships. This is problematic insofar as it points out a continual disavowal of masculine queerness as if that is an evil that needs to be conquered and saved by super-straight men.

REFERENCES

Anderson, Carol. 2016. *White Rage: The Unspoken Truth of Our Racial Divide*. New York: Bloomsbury Publishing.

Anderson, Eric. 2011. "Masculinities and Sexualities in Sport and Physical Cultures: Three Decades of Evolving Research," *Journal of Homosexuality*, 58, no. 5, pp. 565–78.

Ashcraft, Karen Lee, and Mumby, Dennis K. 2004. *Reworking Gender: A Feminist Communicology of Organization*. Thousand Oaks: Sage.

Becker, Ron. 2014. "Becoming Bromosexual: Straight Men, Gay Men, and Male Bonding on U.S. TV," in *Reading the Bromance*, edited by Michael DeAngelis, 128–39. Detroit: Wayne State University Press.

Boyle, Karen, and Berridge, Susan. 2014. "I Love You, Man," *Feminist Media Studies* 14, no. 3, pp. 353–68.

Collins, Patricia Hill. 2000. "Gender, Black Feminism, and Black Political Economy," *The Annals of the American Academy* 568, no. 1, pp. 41–53.

Coyne, Sarah M., Linder, Jennifer Ruth, Rasmussen, Eric E., Nelson, David A., and Collier, Kevin M. 2014. "It's a Bird! It's a Plane! It's a Gender Stereotype!: Longitudinal Associations between Superhero Viewing and Gender Stereotyped Play," *Sex Roles* 70, pp. 416–30.

Crenshaw, Carrie. 1997. "Women in the Gulf War: Toward an Intersectional Feminist Rhetorical Criticism," *Howard Journal of Communications* 8, no. 3, pp. 219–35.

DeAngelis, Michael (Ed). 2014. *Reading the Bromance*. Detroit: Wayne State University Press.

DiAngelo, Robin. 2018. *White Fragility: Why It's so Hard for White People to Talk about Racism*. Boston: Beacon Press.

Doty, Alexander. 1993. *Making Things Perfectly Queer: Interpreting Mass Culture*. Minneapolis: University of Minnesota Press.

Drushel, Bruce E. 2014. "Friends of *Batman* (And Dorothy): Queering the *Green Hornet* Television Series," in *Reading the Bromance*, edited by Michael DeAngelis, 257–68. Detroit: Wayne State University Press.

Ellis, James. 2015. "The Kato Show: Bruce Lee as the Green Hornet's Sidekick," *Newsweek*, November 20, 2015. https://www.newsweek.com/bruce-lee-king-fu-martial-arts-390811.

Feil, Ken. 2014. "From Batman to I Love You, Man: Queer Taste, Vulgarity, and the Bromance as Sensibility and Film Genre," in *Reading the Bromance*, edited by Michael DeAngelis, 93–106. Detroit: Wayne State University Press.

Flannery, Kaitlin M., and Smith, Rhiannon. 2017. "The Effects of Age, Gender, and Gender Role Ideology on Adolescent's Social Perspective-Taking Ability and Tendency in Friendships," *Journal of Social and Personal Relationships*, 34, no. 5, pp. 617–35.

Firth, Hannah, Raisborough, Jayne, and Klein, Orly. 2010. "C'mon Girlfriend," *International Journal of Cultural Studies,* 13, no. 5 pp. 471–89.

Gambacorta, Daniel, and Ketelaar, Timothy. 2013. "Dominance and Deference: Men Inhibit Creative Displays during Mate Competition When Their Competitor Is Strong." *Evolution and Human Behavior,* 34, pp. 330–33.

Moon, Dreama G., and Nakayama, Thomas K. 2005. "Strategic Social Identities and Judgments: A Murder in Appalachia," *Howard Journal of Communication,* 16, no. 2, pp. 87–107.

Nakayama, Thomas K. 1994. "Show/Down Time: "Race," Gender, Sexuality, and Popular Culture," *Critical Studies in Mass Communication,* 11, no. 2, pp. 162–79.

Nardi, Peter M. (Ed.) 1992. *Men's Friendships.* Thousand Oaks, CA: Sage.

Nettleton, Pamela Hill. 2016. "No Girls Allowed: Television Boys' Clubs as Resistance to Feminism," *Television & New Media,* 17, no. 7, pp. 563–78.

Sedgwick, Eve Kosofsky. 1985. *Between Men: English Literature and Male Homosocial Desire.* New York: Columbia University Press.

Shyminsky, Neil. 2011. "'Gay Sidekicks' Queer Anxiety and the Narrative Straightening of the Superhero," *Men and Masculinities,* 14, no. 3, pp. 288–308.

Spangler, Lynn C. 1992. "Buddies and Pals: A History of Male Friendships on Prime-Time Television," in *Men, Masculinity, and the Media,* edited by Steve Craig, 93–110. Newbury Park, CA: Sage.

Urbaniak, Geoffrey, C. and Kilmann, Peter, R. 2003. "Physical Attractiveness and the 'Nice Guy Parodox': Do Nice Guys Really Finish Last?" *Sex Roles,* 49, no. 9–10, pp. 413–26.

Van Vugt, Mark, De Cremer, David, and Dirk P. Janssen. 2007. "Gender Differences in Cooperation and Competition: The Male Warrior Hypothesis," *Psychological Science,* 18, no. 1, pp. 19–23.

Wajcman, Judy. 2010. "Feminist Theories of Technology," *Cambridge Journal of Economics,* 34, no. 1, pp. 143–52.

Wood, Julia T., and Inman, Christopher C. 1993. "In a Different Mode: Masculine Styles of Communicating Closeness," *Journal of Applied Communication Research,* 21, no. 3, pp. 279–95.

Wood, Robin. 2003. *Hollywood from Vietnam to Reagan . . . and Beyond.* New York: Columbia University Press.

Chapter Two

If She Be Worthy

*Performance of Female Masculinity and
Toxic Geek Masculinity in Jason Aaron's*
Thor: The Goddess of Thunder

Hailey J. Austin

The Marvel character Thor was canonically male until 2014 when a masked female picked up his hammer and was worthy of his title and powers. Jane Foster, a side character and love interest to the main character since the beginning of the comic series, became Thor when the original Thor Odinson became unworthy of his name and trademark hammer. While female characters have taken up the mantles of male heroes in superhero comics before, their names are usually changed to more female-centered designations like Supergirl or Spider-Woman. Jane Foster, however, retained the name Thor and was not Lady Thor or Thor Girl. And, perhaps more importantly, she was not hypersexualized. Unlike the female superheroes that came before her, Jane Foster's Thor was fully clothed with bulging biceps instead of bulging breasts. Her Thor was different and, thus, encouraged a new female readership in Marvel's superhero comics. While inspiring to some, the new Thor was seen as threatening to others. Some fans took to the internet to voice their dismay and anger that a woman could be worthy of Thor's hammer, and that she could be as powerful if not more powerful than the male Thor.[1] When the comic was successful and outsold the male Thor, some fans created hate groups online that targeted female comics creators, characters, and fans. The message they conveyed was that women are neither welcome in comics nor worthy of comics culture.

Unlike the male Odinson, the female Thor wears a mask to conceal her identity, reinforcing the masculine performance of superheroes. The mask allows the female Thor access into previously unattainable spaces, namely the masculine superhero space in which she performs female masculinity. Similarly, some male fans use the internet and their usernames as masks through which to perform their toxic geek masculinity as a response to this female Thor's performance. The negative response from some male fans was the result of the misrecognition of gender's connection to power. The new female Thor did not operate as a typical female in superhero comics. Her female masculinity upset the expectations of some male fans because they felt that they could no longer relate to the comic's protagonist. Instead, they related to the male Odinson's unworthiness and symbolic castration. This in turn caused a toxic geek response, in which masculinity was asserted through online threats of violence against women. This chapter will deconstruct the ways in which the performativity of the superhero is revealed through Jane Foster's female masculinity and how this, in turn, has evoked performative and toxic responses from some male fans.

GENDER AS PERFORMANCE

Famously, Judith Butler's *Gender Trouble* (1990) posited that gender itself is a repeated performance: "such acts, gestures, [and] enactments, generally construed, are performative in the sense that the essence or identity that they otherwise purport to express are fabrications manufactured and sustained through corporeal signs and other discursive means" (173). These fabricated corporeal signs are realized and performed as gender, which has traditionally been confined to the binary, cisgender arrangement of male and female. Someone considered male has features commonly associated with masculinity and females embody what are considered to be feminine traits. Such tropes are expressed in superhero comics, where the characters often possess hypersignifiers of their genders. The reception and power afforded to each gender, however, is different. Queer theorist Jack Halberstam[2] (1998) claims "masculinity in this society inevitably conjures up notions of power and legitimacy and privilege" (2). Masculinity has been considered exclusively male as it is tied to a representation of power. Both Sigmund Freud (1905) and Jacques Lacan (1949) considered masculinity an inherently male trait. Halberstam (2002) offers a pragmatic reading of Freud in which the latter "talks about the phallic power as the representation of power that seems to be available to men in social and political terms in a male-dominated culture" (355). In this regard, Freud (1905) finds that a penis generates social power. In his chapter on the mirror stage Lacan (1949) also, perhaps unconsciously, linked the phallus to a representation of self, and thus, power in that the superior male body produces male power. Masculinity, then, has been treated as a power only available to men through their penises.

Butler, on the other hand, regards gender as performative which enables masculinity (and thus power) to be transferred to female bodies. She demonstrates that neither Lacan, through his projection of the idealized body as the locus of control, nor Freud can conceive of a powerful female masculinity (Butler 1993, 73). Similarly to Freud and Lacan, Michel Foucault posits in *The History of Sexuality* (1980) that power is exercised exclusively over life and that "bio-power" is linked to institutional power over the discipline of the body, as well as the power to foster life or destroy it. In his study of Foucault and masturbation, Steve Garlick (2013) finds that the "concern with masturbation was not merely with individual behaviour; rather, it was directed towards the regulation of life itself as it circulated through the bodies of masturbators" (54). Though Garlick (2013) does not gender the bodies in his study, Foucault and the antimasturbation campaigners focused on male masturbation. Garlick (2013) goes on to argue that "men's bodies appear as prominent sites for [. . .] biopolitics" because normative forms of masculinity "attempt to organize a population of sub-individual elements into a coherent and controlled form in order to stake a claim to power" (65). Foucault's (1980) treatment of "bio-power" is male-oriented and, as Donna Haraway (2004) argues, "flaccid" (8). Like Freud and Lacan's theories, Foucault is unable to imagine a female or feminine representation of power.

While there are multiple versions of masculinity that can be performed, toxic masculinity is "the most extreme versions of hyper masculine communities of practice [. . .] characterised by homophobia and the domination and subjugation of weaker men and women" (Creighton and Oliffe 2010, 414–15). Just as the performances of hypermasculine and feminine characterizations and bodies are inherent in superhero comics, so, too, is there a specific performance of toxic masculinity. Comics readership is not free from such idealized depictions of toxic masculinity. Anastasia Salter and Bridget Blodgett (2017) coin the term "toxic geek masculinity" where "representations of men are shaped and defined in relationship to women as other" in online or geek forums that they believe to be exclusively male (13). While geeks are not the societal ideal of masculinity, "geeks either play or are encouraged to identify with the hero. Popular culture reinforces the connection between geeks and heroic icons, particularly superheroes" (Salter and Blodgett 2017, 9). The superhero genre often shows a duality in which the hero is a geek by day but uses his smarts or technology to become a hero at night. This resonates with geek fans. However, with comic book industries attempting to include diverse characters of different races, genders, and sexualities, the white male geek readers no longer see *only* themselves in superhero comics. This has generated a negative response, leading some men to perform toxic geek masculinity through online interactions that emphasize maintaining straight white male-centered comics rather than diversifying the superhero genre.

Social media usernames and the faceless nature of the internet are a kind of performativity in and of themselves. According to Butler (1997),

> the speech act, as a rite of institution, is one whose contexts are never fully determined in advance, and that the possibility for the speech act to take on a non-ordinary meaning, to function in contexts where it has not belonged, is precisely the political promise of the performative, one that positions the performative at the center of a politics of hegemony, one that offers an unanticipated political future for deconstructive thinking. (161)

Performativity through the online "speech act" allows for the creation of an online mask and enables toxic reactions. The fans displaying toxic geek masculinity often call for others to berate female/LGBTQ+ comics creators, editors, and fans. In February 2018, some comics fans released a blacklist of "SJW [Social Justice Warrior] Vipers" for their followers to boycott, the majority of which were women and people of color (Francisco 2018). This boycott spawned from a YouTube video in which a male comics fan and creator, username Diversity & Comics, called one female Marvel editor a "cum-dumpster" and accused various female writers of "sucking their way into the industry" (Elbein 2018). In doing so, a movement against female comics creators, editors, and fans called "Comicsgate" was created and perpetuated. The comics readers' masculinity is performed in a toxic way and is formulated through "eroticized male dominance and female submission" (Gardiner 2009, 623). While it inherently forces itself upon others, it is important to note that toxic masculinity is also forced upon the person in power. An integral part of the description of toxic masculinity lies in its rigid and hierarchical definition of masculinity conflated with power that diminishes and/or oppresses others. However, this also creates an untenable, toxic idealized form of masculinity that can result in physical, biological, and psychological deterioration in the empowered male. This toxic performativity is linked to a male narcissism: "To the extent that they are unable to access the power they feel has been reserved for them, men tend to project their own misrecognition of the relationship between penises and male power onto the world around them" (Halberstam 2002, 357). A failure to recognize the performativity of gender has led to male masculinity being the societal, and consequently superhero, default. Attempts to diversify the genre through characters like Jane Foster's Thor have resulted in toxic masculine responses that threaten female characters, creators, and fans.

THE QUEER MASCULINE FEMININE OF THOR

In order to consider the impact of Jane Foster's Thor, it is necessary to give a brief history of both characters. In 1962, the mythological Norse god of thunder, Thor, debuted in Marvel Comics' *Journey into Mystery #83* by Stan Lee, Larry Lieber, and Jack Kirby. In the comics, Thor is the Asgardian god of thunder whose enchanted hammer, Mjolnir, gives him super strength, the power to manipulate the weather, and the ability to fly by twirling the hammer. Originally, the immortal god of thunder coinhabited the body of mortal Dr. Donald Blake. The story switched between the two bodies and personalities, eventually creating a love triangle with Dr. Blake's assistant Jane Foster. One of the main elements of the superhero's mythos is his hammer, Mjolnir. Thor's father, Odin, bestowed it upon his son with the engraving, "Whosoever holds this hammer, if he be worthy, shall possess the power of Thor." With this wording and over fifty years of storyline, twelve characters have been worthy enough to wield the hammer, including a horse-faced alien and a frog (Schedeen 2014). Canonically, none of them had been female.[3]

Before 2014, Jane Foster was an all-but unknown side character. Though she first appeared in *Journey into Mystery* #84, one issue after Thor, Jane Foster had most commonly been depicted as a supporting character or love interest for Thor. In her first appearance, Jane Foster was a nurse employed by Dr. Blake, before becoming a doctor herself in later installments. In the original storyline when Thor revealed that he and Dr. Blake were the same person, Thor took Jane to Asgard with him. There, Jane was granted immortality until she failed to pass Odin's tests of courage. Odin then strips her of her powers and memory, returning her to Earth. The character became more well-known after being played by Natalie Portman in Marvel's *Thor* (2011) film. In this adaptation, she is a world-leading astrophysicist and astronomer.

In Jason Aaron's first run of Thor in *Thor: God of Thunder* (2012), Jane Foster is an ambassador, Thor's ex-lover, and in the advanced stages of breast cancer. Jane Foster became a hero in her own right in 2014 when she picked up the mantle of Thor, even though every time she lifts the hammer it undoes the effects of her chemotherapy. Aaron introduced her as Thor after the male Odinson, whom Aaron began writing in 2012, had been made unworthy. In Aaron's *Original Sin* (2014), Nick Fury, the leader of the Agents of S.H.I.E.L.D., whispered something inaudible in Thor Odinson's ear which caused him to be unworthy and drop the hammer on the moon. The words that rendered Thor Odinson unworthy were not revealed until *The Unworthy Thor #5* (2017). Fury whispered, "Gorr was right," referencing the villain in Aaron's first Thor comics (Aaron 2017 #5, 16). Gorr was a time-traveler known as the God Butcher who believed that all gods should be killed because they do not actually help people. Odinson becomes unworthy when people believe the gods are selfish and only help themselves: a theme that is revisited with Jane Foster's Thor.

At the end of the first issue of the female Thor's storyline, an unknown female figure, later revealed to be Jane Foster, walks on the moon and whispers, "there must always be a Thor" and grips the handle of the hammer

(Aaron 2014, #1, 22). The final panel shows Mjolnir's inscription has been rewritten by the lightning Thor now controls to "if *she* be worthy." This is significant not only in that Jane is the first female worthy of Thor's powers, but in the fact that she retains the traditionally male name. According to Aaron, "you pick up this book and it just says 'Thor' on the cover, which features a new female version of Thor. It's pretty much telling you she's not She-Thor or Lady Thor. She's not Thorika. She is Thor. This is the new Thor" (Richards 2014).

Jane Foster's characterization as a side character was a common fate for females in superhero comics. According to comics artist and scholar Trina Robbins (2013), female superheroes and strong females in comics have historically been scarce:

> This was the plight of most comic book action heroines. None had ever appeared in her own book, and they were invariably short-lived, rarely lasting for more than three appearances before fading into permanent obscurity. Often they were merely sidekicks of the more important male hero. For the most part, when women appeared in comics they were relegated to the role of girlfriend, and their purpose was to be rescued by the hero. Girl readers could find little in the way of heroic role models in the pages of comic books. (54)

Even when they are successful characters, many female superheroes are (or are marketed as) female versions of male heroes. Salter and Blodgett (2017) find that while superbodies within comics are able to push past human limitations and are limited only to the artists' imagination, "superbodies rarely explore liminal spaces or offer new ways to conceptualize gender or strength. Instead, they often fall into predictable and stereotyped patterns of a fetishized ideal" (110). Because of this, female characters in superhero comics have been drawn, represented, and characterized differently from their male counterparts. For example, Batgirl and Spider-Woman are derivative of Batman and Spider-Man. The feminine designation of their names is expounded with their use as plot devices and their hypersexualized appearances. For instance, in Alan Moore's *The Killing Joke* (1988), Barbara Gordon (Batgirl) is shot, crippled, and sexually assaulted by the Joker in order to motivate her father, Commissioner Gordon, toward revenge.

The use of female death and mutilation to motivate a male character has unfortunately become a recognizable comic book trope. On the website "Women in Refrigerators," female comic writer Gail Simone (2000) coined the term "fridging" after an incident in *Green Lantern* #54 (1994) in which the title hero comes home to find that his girlfriend was killed and stuffed into the refrigerator. Simone (2000), along with a group of fellow feminists and comic fans, created the website to highlight the amount of times female comics characters are injured, killed, or disempowered as a plot device. The site found that while not all female comics characters had been "killed, raped, depowered, crippled, turned evil, maimed, tortured, contracted a disease or had other life-derailing tragedies befall her," the 111 characters in the list made it hard to think of exceptions ("Women in Refrigerators" 2000). The list and website were meant to raise awareness of fridging, opening up the discussion to creators and fans alike. Women in comics were not only questioning the treatment of female characters within the superhero genre but pushing back against their hyperfeminized and hypersexualized treatment. Jane Foster's Thor raised awareness of these tropes, prompted an often-toxic response, and eventually succumbed to the fate of the female superhero by being fridged at the end of her run.

Jane Foster's Thor performs a female masculinity and, in doing so, reveals the overt gender performativity within superhero comics. According to Halberstam (2002), "female masculinity [. . .] disrupts contemporary cultural studies accounts of masculinity within which masculinity always boils down to the social, cultural and political effects of male embodiment and male privilege" (345). Female masculinity is not the imitation of maleness, but instead questions the legitimacy of masculinity's association with only maleness and thus power. In superhero comics, "feminization is very directly equated to deprecation of value" (Salter and Blodgett 2017, 104). However, the female Thor's performance of female masculinity exposes the disproportionate powers and privileges afforded to men due to social, cultural, and political associations of masculinity. She performs masculinity through her appearance: largely through her mask, two different identities, and costume. Many studies have focused on defining masculinity as a masquerade and the superhero genre exemplifies these conjectures (Perchuk and Posner 1995). On top of the fact that it evokes a visual spectacle, the mask of a superhero creates a power dynamic in which the wearer is in control of who knows their identity. According to Friedrich Weltzien (2015), "As a very special kind of dress the mask always provokes the wish to see behind it, to take it off and to discover something hidden" (230). The mask also allows the wearer to seamlessly access spaces that they may have been prohibited from before without their true identity being discovered. This gives the figure a special authority over others. In the comics, the female Thor is masked while the male Odinson is not. The mask, as part of her uniform and transformation into an Asgardian god, enables Thor to fly through space to other worlds she could not before as a human. It also affords her the authority and power she does not have as Jane Foster the ambassador. Without her mask, she does not have her powers and is expected to be a peaceful ambassador in the public sphere. With her mask, however, Thor is allowed and even prompted to solve things in a violent manner.

The female Thor's dual identities not only reference the dual identities of Thor and Dr. Blake in the original Thor comics, but by having them, she performs a kind of masculinity. Weltzien (2015) identifies what he calls a "heroic metamorphic masculinity" in the superhero's transformation between their private life and their public heroic identity as it "is always indicated by the change of clothes" (232). The performance and masquerade aspects of gender are equivalent to the wearing of clothes which, in and of itself, signifies social codes rather than a biological or psychological reality. When Jane Foster picks up the hammer, her clothes change from her human garb to the warrior wear of The Mighty Thor. This costume evokes a gladiator and superhero tradition: "Superhero costumes are inventions of comic-book authors but refer to a tradition of the appearance of warriors and sportsmen that might be seen as emphasizing masculinity" (Weltzien 2015, 236). It is also, more importantly, a performance akin to the male superhero performance. The female Thor is performing masculinity through her dress and dual identity just as the male superheroes do in order to gain access to the masculine space of the superhero rather than the hypersexualized role of the female superhero who is only allowed to operate in feminine spaces.

Female characters using clothing to gain entrance into exclusively male spaces is a trope seen in real life and other forms of literature as well. Different deployments of cross-dressing appear in novels and plays throughout history in ways that have allowed female characters to access the privileges of the male space. According to Tina O'Toole (2013), Irish New Woman texts in the eighteenth century were the "introduction of untraditional or transgressive role models for women" in literature (110). In this tradition, "the Boy was one avenue through which they could access male privilege, at least temporarily" and "on a more playful level, gender swap gave the Boy the chance to dispense with women's constrictive costume and to play with the props of masculinity" (O'Toole 2013, 110–11). So, too, has the female Thor revealed an "untraditional" role for women in comics in that she is a superheroine performing female masculinity with the name and title of a powerful male character. She has also been given the ability to utilize the masculine prop of the hammer, which allows her access to realms and powers she was not allowed before. Sandra Gilbert and Susan Gubar (1979) argue that the "pen is in some sense (even more figuratively) a penis" (4). Similarly, it could be argued that the hammer, much like the sword or pen, is a phallic image of power. The male Odinson's unworthiness and inability to lift the hammer, then, is a sign of impotence or castration in that "a man who loses or abuses such power become like a eunuch—or like a woman" (Gilbert and Gubar 1979, 10). In the case of Jason Aaron's *Thor*, the female Thor performs the masculine and wields Mjolnir while Odinson remains castrated or feminized by a whisper from Nick Fury, forcing him to drop the hammer.

The ideas presented by Gilbert and Gubar, however, are based in the male-centered power theories of Freud (1905), Lacan (1949), and Foucault (1980). Butler (1993) and Halberstam (2002) reveal a power structure in which male does not mean masculine, thus providing a more nuanced approach to the analysis of the female Thor's power and Odinson's unworthiness. Butler (1993) notes a slip in Freud's (1905) distinction between the penis and phallic power, stressing that in today's society there is "transferability of the phallus" (57). Butler (1993) directly confronts and disrupts the notion that masculinity can only be displayed by male bodies. Instead, women can possess traits that have been traditionally seen as exclusively male. A female Thor is worthy of wielding a masculine object, often better than her male predecessor, without being sexualized. But, instead of a castration, Halberstam (2002) suggests that,

> In the age of viagra and penile enlargements, we might argue, male sexuality and male masculinity in general tends to be a mediated affair in all kinds of situations, and the apparent fragility of erectile function might stand as a symbol for other kinds of masculine vulnerabilities that move far beyond the psychoanalytic formulation of castration anxiety. (353–54)

In modern society, the fear of an inability to perform sexually is much more relevant than castration anxiety. In the case of Thor and Odinson, the female is able to perform while the male is not. Odinson, then, is no longer emasculated or feminized, but could instead be read as jealous of the female Thor's ability to perform: masculinity, sexually, or otherwise. When read as the inability to perform, female masculinity changes from a woman performing as a man to questioning the performance of masculinity as a strictly male venture.

TOXIC MALE REACTIONS TO FEMALE THOR

While Butler (1993) demonstrates that neither Lacan (1949) nor Freud (1905) can conceive of a powerful female masculinity, a portion of the male comic book fans responded to it with toxic geek masculinity. They took to social media and the fan response pages of the comics to voice their discontent, often calling the female Thor a gimmick to attract women to the medium. Though the names of these fans are known, they will be referred to by their usernames in order to emphasize the performative nature of their speech. In his blog "Jason Aaron: God of Blunders," the blogger Toy Soldiers (2015) argues, "Pandering to the feminist demographic does not move books. It does, however, insult the existing fan base, engage in pandering and misandry, and fuels more antagonisms between fans and feminists." His speech appears to instantiate a binary between feminists and fans, suggesting, in a false dichotomy, that someone cannot be both. He also asserts that feminist tropes do not sell comics. In reality, the female Thor did move books and was extremely successful. According to Comichron (2014), female *Thor #1* (2014) sold over 166,217 copies and was the third best-selling comic that month. It outsold both Aaron's *Thor: God of Thunder #1* (2012), which sold 111,600 copies, as well as Aaron's newest *Thor #1* (2018) in the reset back to the male Thor, which sold 102,530 copies (Comichron 2012 and 2018).[4] Toy Soldiers (2015) goes on to argue that Aaron proves critics of feminism, who "think feminism is about taking away men's power, masculinity, and identity and giving those to women," correct by taking "away Thor's power, masculinity, identity, and his very name and giv[ing] it to a woman who promptly wields them to humiliate Thor and show he was never worthy of any of them to begin with." This reaction reveals a toxic geek masculinity in which the blogger identifies with Odinson and feels that a female Thor is humiliating and emasculating him personally by simply existing in a masculine space. Toy Soldiers (2015) is unable to accept the female masculinity of Jane Foster's Thor. However, as Halberstam (1998) argues, all female masculinity, "actually affords us a glimpse of how masculinity is constructed as masculinity" (1). Thor's performance of masculinity reveals that masculinity itself is, in fact, a performance that is loosely held together by social constructs. This in turn can cause unease in readers who believe their masculinity is linked to their maleness and, thus, power.

While Aaron responded to these types of fans in interviews, he also began writing an even more masculine and feminist Thor in each issue. In the fifth issue, the female Thor is fighting the villain Absorbing Man who says, "Thor? Are you kidding me? I'm supposed to call you Thor? Damn feminists are ruining everything!" (Aaron 2014 #5, 4). Thor later breaks his jaw with her hammer, thinking, "That's for saying 'feminist' like it's a four-letter word, creep" (Aaron 2014 #5, 5). The female Thor later combats Odinson who accuses her of stealing his hammer and demands, "Unhand my hammer, woman. Or know the wrath of Thor" (Aaron 2014 #3, 20). Unlike some male fans, who could not grapple with a female Thor being worthy, Thor Odinson recants after seeing Mjolnir fly for Jane Foster. In fact, he even goes so far as to say, "I am not worthy of it. I am still the Prince of Asgard. I am still [. . .] Odinson. But she is Thor now," literally giving her his name (Aaron 2014 #4, 18).

"Comicsgate" was created in order to voice certain fans' opinions on diverse comics creators and characters through online abuse and the boycotting of certain titles. It began when a group of female Marvel editors and staff posted a photo of themselves drinking milkshakes to celebrate the legacy of female comics publisher Flo Steinberg, who had died five days before. The women received scores of online abuse calling them "fake geek girls," "social justice warriors," "tumblr-virtue signallers," and they were accused of ruining the comics industry with their very presence (Elbein 2018). Part of the reason women in particular have been targeted with these toxic responses is because they are viewed as Others and outside the definition of geek or fan. According to Salter and Blodgett (2017), "Feminists, social justice warriors, and critics become easy targets for geeks' own unhappiness with their communities and lives [. . .] women and minority groups can't be part of these communities because even thinking about them as participants breaks the image of the geek as solitary, disliked male" (202). The abuse continued, devolving into more targeted harassment and death threats, leading at least one editor to leave Marvel Comics all together. The followers of "Comicsgate" continue to berate and attack female and LGBTQ+ creators and characters, blaming them for the political nature of comics they no longer enjoy.

One of the proprietors of the "Comicsgate" movement is the ironically titled handle Diversity & Comics.[5] His YouTube videos are a mixture of reviews, analysis, and his opinions on current online battles in the comics community. His videos are exceedingly performative; he never shows his face, refers to himself by the false name Zak,[6] and often physically rips apart comics he does not agree with. In doing so, he uses the internet and his online handle as a mask through which to perform his toxic masculinity. Every video exemplifies his belief that "the failures of the comics industry were a direct result of hiring diverse talent, and that they need to be driven out" (Elbein 2018). His lexicon and method of harassment was inspired by the 2014 "Gamergate," in which female videogame creators and critics were publicly harassed and blamed for ruining the videogame industry. Diversity & Comics as well as other geek-correlated groups, such as the Men's Rights Activists and antifeminists, use the term Social Justice Warrior to identify the characters, creators, and fans who they view as feminist, political, and/or illegitimate. In his video titled "Marvel GENERATIONS Gently Reminds Fans That SJW Thor Is Just As Good As Real Thor (but better)," Diversity & Comics (2017) claims the comic

> is intended to show that fake Thor, SJW Thor, Jane Foster's Thor, Lady Thor, is better than the actual Thor whose name is Thor because he's Thor. [. . .] You can call her "Lady Thor: Goddess of Thunder." That's fine. I wouldn't argue that. You wanna say that she's Thor? She's not Thor.

Diversity & Comics repeatedly delegitimizes the female Thor, calling her fake and denying her agency and worthiness. The only way he feels she could be legitimate is if she were to have the same name subordination as the female superheroes before her, operating in a female space and not threatening the male space. Because she shares Thor's name and powers, he finds her threatening and inauthentic. Halberstam (2002) argues that while "masculinity depicts itself quite simply as real masculinity, it simultaneously exhibits some anxiety about the status of its own realness: male masculinity as an identity seems to demand authentication" (353). In this case, Diversity & Comics demands authentication of a male masculinity instead of a female with the same powers and name. In order to feel validated, Diversity &

Comics uses his handle as an online performance in an attempt to reassert his masculinity in light of perceived threats and to have his masculinity recognized by others in an online space.

Similarly, Diversity & Comics goes on to note the size of the female Thor's arms, saying, "I've not found this in real life. I've not found these women who constantly want to be men and constantly want to compete with them and replace them[. . . .] Her arms are not actually as big as his, but considering the difference between men and women, she's above average and he's about average for a hero" (2017). He is quick to point out the female masculinity Thor embodies, but is frustrated that she is depicted as performing masculinity "better" than the male Thor. This reveals the ways in which the "viability and suppression of female masculinity concerns forms of male narcissism that allow men to misrecognize their penises as proof of their superiority and guarantor of their privileged relations to power, language, sexuality, desire" (Halberstam 2002, 356–57). Diversity & Comics' argument reveals his misrecognition of the power and privilege of maleness. He claims that because he has not encountered it in his personal experience, female masculinity can be delegitimized and othered. Like Freud (1905), Lacan (1949), and Foucault (1980), he is unable to imagine a powerful female masculinity or Butler's (1993) transferability of the phallus. Instead, his argument reveals a belief that Thor's performance of masculinity is a performance of male power. His toxic geek response to this perceived threat is to use his online mask to assert his masculinity onto female characters, creators, and fans alike.

In an interview with *The Daily Beast,* the Diversity & Comics creator explained that he began to see a change in comics that annoyed him: "feminization of men, masculinization of women, basically, all the classic heterosexual pairings being destroyed" (Elbein 2018). His toxic response to these changes suggests a fear of legitimizing his own masculinity as well as maintaining heteronormativity. The fear of representations of female masculinity in comics is not a new phenomenon. It is a dated argument that was popularized in the 1950s by psychologist Fredric Wertham whose *Seduction of the Innocent* (1954) led to industry self-censorship with the Comics Code Authority. Wertham (1954) argued that comics played into a climate of sexual anxieties that corrupted juveniles. He was most vehement toward Wonder Woman who he considered "physically very powerful, tortures men, has her own female following, is the cruel 'phallic' woman. While she is a frightening figure for boys, she is an undesirable ideal for girls, being the exact opposite of what girls are supposed to be" (This 2014, 30). Like Diversity & Comics, Wertham (1954) felt that female masculinity went against the standard feminine roles that women were supposed to follow. He also argued that "For boys, Wonder Woman is a frightening image. For girls she is a morbid ideal. Where Batman is anti-feminine, the attractive Wonder Woman and her counterparts are definitely anti-masculine" (Wertham 1954, 192–93). Both Wonder Woman and Jane Foster's Thor are powerful females that perform masculinity within comics, and both Wertham and Diversity & Comics find their combination of femininity and masculinity frightening because it is not heteronormative, and thus, threatens their male power.

Diversity & Comics fervently purports heteronormativity and gender roles saying, "Men are not women and women are not men. Women do not have fantasies about fighting, especially women in the medical field. I think eventually Jane Foster became a doctor" (2017). He denies any kind of female masculinity or gender fluidity and cites this, as well as her sex, as a reason for believing the female Thor is inauthentic. For him, fighting is a masculine trait and thus exclusively male. Similarly, Halberstam notes in the conclusion to *Female Masculinity* (1998) that boxing provides a metaphor for the power of dominant masculinities, as absorbing blows in boxing "is not unlike the structure of white male masculinity, which seems impervious to criticism or attack and maintains hegemonic sway despite all challenges to its power" (275). In the comics, Jane Foster's Thor both gives and receives punches, often inflicting more damage than she takes. Because she performs a masculinity that reveals a masculine anxiety, Jane Foster's Thor threatens the legitimacy of masculine power and heteronormative gender roles themselves. Though it is easy to vilify Diversity & Comics and other "Comics-gate" participants, it is important to remember that toxic geek masculinity is performative. Halberstam (1998) states that "compulsory masculinity is a burden on many different kinds of men and boys" but it is hard to consider this burden because "it so often expresses itself through the desire to destroy others, often women" (274). But fighting, and overcoming toxic masculinity, is something female superheroes are required to do. Similarly, female fans and creators have had to overcome immense levels of toxic geek masculinity and online hate in order to exist in the male-centered comics culture.

THOR'S LEGACY AND
REVERSION TO THE FEMALE SPACE

Even though she successfully performed masculinity, the female Thor was not exempt from the fate shared by a majority of females in superhero comics: being turned into a plot device. In Aaron's storyline, the human Jane Foster is dying from breast cancer and every time she changes into Thor, her chemotherapy treatments are undone, leaving her sicker than before. Ultimately, her cancer acts as a means through which she can be fridged or used to further the plot for the male Thor Odinson. The "Death of Mighty Thor" storyline (2018) features Jane Foster sacrificing herself and Mjolnir to save Asgardia from the Mangog, a villain like Gorr who believed the gods should be punished for not helping people. Because Jane Foster is a mortal, she is able to defeat the Mangog. Her sacrifice motivates Thor Odinson to take up his original mantle. In the end, Odin spares Jane Foster from death, but with no Mjolnir with which to be worthy, she is sent back to the hospital to undergo chemotherapy. The male Odinson then regains the mantle of Thor in *Thor #1* (2018), resetting the storyline back to the straight white male hero, and the status quo. Even though Jane Foster was able to retain her female masculinity and worthiness for four years, she was ultimately unable to overcome the institutional, male-centeredness of the comics industry and fandom. She was reverted back to her secondary role: stripped of her powers and the mask that allowed her to operate in the traditionally male space. This gives the impression that fans with toxic responses to the character were victorious. Eliminating a character who refused to conform to gender stereotypes purports the idea that superheroes and their power is only available for men.

Though Jane Foster's character is still present in the current comics, she no longer performs female masculinity. In the 2019 Marvel event *The War of the Realms*, the Valkyries (an all-female group of Pegasus-riding warrior goddesses) are all killed defending the Earth. Thor's mother Freya names Jane Foster as the All-Mother of Asgardia (Aaron 2019, #2, 21). As the All-Mother, Jane Foster is given power that is only available to women. This power, which is almost certainly less than that of the All-Father, does not threaten the masculinity of the readers nor demonstrate that gender is performative. Later, it was announced that Jane Foster would get her own series, *Jane Foster: Valkyrie* (Frevele 2019). While many fans are excited for the return of Jane Foster as a flying hero, her role as a Valkyrie only maintains the narrative that females do not belong in male superhero spaces. Instead of taking up and retaining the mantle and name of a male hero, the female Thor was depowered and fridged. Perhaps because of the negative male response to her female masculinity, Jane Foster is only allowed to operate as a hero in an exclusively female and largely feminine space. She is no longer worthy of access to the male superhero space.

Fridging the character and relegating her to a female-only space has returned the comics to the male-centered status quo. It has also demonstrated that the current comics culture rejects Butler's (1993) dynamic transferability of the phallus. And instead, reasserts Freud (1905), Lacan (1949), and Foucault's (1980) male-only power structure which does not allow for gender to be recognized as a performance. For now, the hammer, the phallus, and the power remain in the hands of male characters, creators, and fans. Marvel may have increased their sales and brought in new female readers, however, by rendering the female Thor a temporary plot device they have cultivated a comics culture that encourages further toxic responses to females and female heroes. To combat this, more strong female comics characters, who are not fridged or sexualized, are needed. Fans and creators should demand more empowered female representation that is not used as a love interest, plot device, or novelty character. Once characters who challenge heteronormativity are the norm then perhaps the social perception of female masculinity will not devolve into toxic masculinity. Women have been and continue to be involved in comics despite fridging and online harassment. Until systemic changes are made to include female characters, creators, and fans in superhero comics, their worthiness will remain a source of debate in comics fandoms and comics studies.

NOTES

1. While I devote a full section in this essay to investigate some extreme examples, it will here suffice to say that there is a litany of examples that can be found through a basic internet search on the topic.
2. Previously "Judith Halberstam" in his publications.
3. The one instance in which a female was worthy was a DC/Marvel crossover event that was not considered canon. In a battle royale-type event, readers could vote on who would win in fights between DC and Marvel characters. DC's Wonder Woman was worthy of Mjolnir, but she put the hammer down before fighting X-Men's Storm. See David et al. (1996).
4. These numbers reflect those preordered from comic book stores and does not include those bought by customers in store or online. In this sense, the numbers reflect the stores' confidence in the book rather than the actual sales numbers, which are not properly recorded.
5. Because he is suing comics creator Mark Waid for defamation, Diversity & Comics has deleted the majority of his social media accounts, including his Twitter (Trent 2018). Likely because of the negative associations with his handle, he has since changed his YouTube username to Comics MATTER w/Ya Boi Zak.
6. His real name is Richard C. Meyer.

REFERENCES

Aaron, Jason, and Esad Ribic. 2013. *Thor, God of Thunder. [1], [1],*. New York: Marvel Worldwide.
Aaron, Jason (writer), Russel Dauterman (artist #1–4), and Jorge Molina (artist #5). 2014. "Thor: The Goddess of Thunder." In *Thor* volume 1 issues #1–5, Marvel Comics.
Aaron, Jason (writer), Olivier Coipel, Kim Jacinto and Pascal Alixe (artists). 2017. *The Unworthy Thor* #5, Marvel Comics.
Aaron, Jason (writer) and Russel Dauterman (artist). 2019. *The War of the Realms* #2, Marvel Comics.
Brubaker, Ed, Javier Pulido (ILT), Mark Waid, Jim Cheung (ILT), Paco Medina (ILT). 2014. *Original Sin*. Marvel Enterprises.
Butler, Judith. 1993. *Bodies That Matter: On the Discursive Limits of "Sex."* New York: Routledge.
Butler, Judith. 1997. *Excitable Speech: A Politics of the Performative*. New York: Routledge.
Butler, Judith. 1990. *Gender Trouble: Feminism and the Subversion of Identity*. New York: Routledge.
Comichron. 2012. "2012 Comic Book Sales to Comics Shops." http://www.comichron.com/monthlycomicssales/2012.html.
Comichron. 2014. "2014 Comic Book Sales to Comics Shops." http://www.comichron.com/monthlycomicssales/2014.html.
Comichron. 2018. "2018 Comic Book Sales to Comics Shops." http://www.comichron.com/monthlycomicssales/2018.html.

Creighton, Genevieve and John L. Oliffe. 2010. "Theorising Masculinities and Men's Health: A Brief History with a View to Practice." *Health Sociology Review* 19.4 (October): 409–18. DOI: https://doi.org/10.5172/hesr.2010.19.4.409.

David, Peter (writer), Claudio Castellini and Dan Jurgens (pencils), Paul Neary and Joe Rubinstein (inks). 1996. *Marvel versus DC* #2, Marvel Comics and DC Comics.

Diversity & Comics. 2017. "Marvel GENERATIONS Gently Reminds Fans That SJW Thor Is Just As Good As Real Thor (but better)." YouTube. Published August 23, 2017. https://www.youtube.com/watch?v=2i8HjRge8Wg.

Elbein, Asher. 2018. "#Comicsgate: How an Anti-Diversity Harassment Campaign in Comics Got Ugly—and Profitable." In *Daily Beast* (April 2nd, 2018) https://www.thedailybeast.com/comicsgate-how-an-anti-diversity-harassment-campaign-in-comics-got-uglyand-profitable.

Foucault, Michel. 1980. *The History of Sexuality Vol 1: An Introduction*. Trans. Robert Hurley. New York: Vintage.

Francisco, Eric. 2018. "Comicsgate Is Gamergate's Next Horrible Evolution." In *Inverse* (February 9, 2018) https://www.inverse.com/article/41132-comicsgate-explained-bigots-milkshake-marvel-dc-gamergate?refresh=44.

Freud, Sigmund. 1991 [1905]. *On Sexuality: Three Essays on the Theory of Sexuality*. London: Penguin.

Frevele, Jamie. 2019. "Jane Foster Is Revealed as the New Valkyrie in This July's New Ongoing Series" Marvel.com. April 18, 2019. https://www.marvel.com/articles/comics/the-new-valkyrie-is-revealed-for-this-july-s-new-series.

Gardiner, Judith Kegan. 2009."Female Masculinities: A Review Essay." *Men and Masculinities* 11.5 (August): 622–33.

Garlick, Steve. 2013. "The Biopolitics of Masturbation: Masculinity, Complexity, and Security." *Body & Society* 20.2 (October): 44–67.

Gilbert, Sandra M., and Susan Gubar. 1979. *The Madwoman in the Attic: The Woman Writer and the Nineteenth-Century Literary Imagination*. New Haven: Yale University Press.

Halberstam, Judith. 1998. *Female Masculinity*. Duke University Press.

Halberstam, Judith. 2002. "The Good, The Bad, and the Ugly: Men, Women, and Masculinity." In *Masculinity Studies and Feminist Theory: New Directions*, 344–67. Edited by Judith Kegan Gardiner. New York: Columbia University Press.

Haraway, Donna. 2004. *The Haraway Reader.* New York: Routledge.

Lacan, Jacques. 1977 [1949]. "The Mirror Stage as Formative of the Function of the I." In *Ecrits: A Selection*. Trans. Alan Sheridan. New York: Norton.

Moore, Alan, Brian Bolland, Richard Starkings, and Tim Sale. 2008. *Batman: the killing joke*.

O'Toole, Tina. 2013. *The New Irish Woman*. United Kingdom: Palgrave Macmillan.

Perchuk, Andrew and Helaine Posner (editors). 1995. *The Masculine Masquerade: Masculinity and Representation*. Cambridge, MA: MIT Press.

Richards, Dave. 2014. "Jason Aaron Explains 'Thor's' New, female God of Thunder," ComicBookResources.com. https://www.cbr.com/jason-aaron-explains-thors-new-female-god-of-thunder/.

Robbins, Trina. 2013. "The Great Women Superheroes." In *The Superhero Reader*, 53–60. Edited by Charles Hatfield, Jeet Heer, and Kent Worcester. University Press of Mississippi.

Salter, Anastasia, and Bridget Blodgett. 2017. *Toxic Geek Masculinity in Media: Sexism, Trolling and Identity Policing*. United Kingdom: Palgrave Macmillan.

Schedeen, Jesse. 2014. "12 Other Characters Who Have Lifted Thor's Hammer Mjolnir." In *IGN*. October 1, 2014. https://in.ign.com/comics/67578/feature/12-other-characters-who-have-lifted-thors-hammer-mjolnir?p=2.

This, Craig. 2014. "Containing Wonder Woman: Fredric Wertham's Battle Against the Mighty Amazon." In *The Ages of Wonder Woman: Essays on the Amazon Princess in Changing Times,* 30–41. Edited by Joseph J. Darowski. Jefferson, NC: McFarland & Company.

Toy Soldiers. 2015. "Jason Aaron: God of Blunders." Wordpress Blog. February 15, 2015. https://toysoldier.wordpress.com/2015/02/15/jason-aaron-god-of-blunders/.

Trent, John F. 2018. "Diversity & Comics Files Lawsuit against Mark Waid after Antarctic Press Dropped Jawbreakers—Lost Souls!" Bounding into Comics. September 29, 2018.

https://boundingintocomics.com/2018/09/29/diversity-comics-files-lawsuit-against-mark-waid-after-antarctic-press-dropped-jawbreakers-lost-souls/.

Weltzien, Friedrich. 2015. "Masque-*ulinities*: Changing Dress as Display of Masculinity in the Superhero Genre." *Fashion Theory* 9.2 (April): 229–50. DOI: 10.2752/136270405778051374.

Wertham, Fredric. 1954. *Seduction of the Innocent*. New York: Rinehart.

"Women in Refrigerators." 2000. Website. https://geekfeminism.wikia.org/wiki/Women_in_refrigerators.

Chapter Three

Witches and Witchbreed in *Marvel 1602*

Kevin Cummings

THE ANOMALIES THAT BIND US

In September 1963, Stan Lee and Jack Kirby introduced the world to mutant superheroes with the release of *X-Men* #1, a comic book centering on individuals with astonishing abilities. The X-Men align themselves with others who share their gift and curse. Together the mutants fight for a world that will allow their kind to live in peace. Mutants possess a genetic X-factor that distinguishes them from normal humans. It also makes them distinct from other superheroes whose powers emerge from accidents, mythic artifacts, or super serums. And, while many heroes hide their identity to protect loved ones from villains, mutants hide their identity because they are persecuted for their differences. As Scott Bukatman (1994) notes, "Mutant powers are stigmata that must be kept hidden from the unreasoning mob of mere mortals" (66). Neil Gaiman's *Marvel 1602* (2003) offers an alternative account of the genesis of the Marvel pantheon of heroes, unmoored from contemporary times and situated instead in the Renaissance. It depicts a time when innocent women were burned at the stake. Presenting mutants as "witchbreed," *Marvel 1602* develops a parallel story of the X-Men, who are hunted during the Inquisition.

Mutant bodies are the subject of much academic research in which they are explicitly analogized to the precarious bodies of women, Jews, Muslims, and refugees (Darowski 2014; Bukatman 1994). Part of the eloquence of Gaiman's meditation on persecution comes from the way he crafts his story about mutants engaging in resistance to toxic prejudices. *Marvel 1602* is a lesson to readers that reveals how mutant identity is governed and how outsiders challenge the dominant order. This essay explores strategies for resistance in Gaiman's narrative by considering how it provides a lens to analyze a particularly virulent form of prejudice that has a historic antecedent in the treatment of witches.

Gaiman, along with artists Andy Kubert and Richard Isanove, won the Quill Award for the best graphic novel in 2005 with their well-crafted "what if" story. But their work also functions as advocacy. It acknowledges the terrible suffering women experienced when they were charged and punished as witches. By some estimates, over 100,000 individuals were killed in Europe and the American colonies from the fifteenth to the eighteenth centuries (Barstow 1994, 23). In addition to revealing the brutality involved in burning women at the stake, Gaiman also reimagines a world where witchbreed forge alliances and find hidden reservoirs of power to challenge repression and injustice. One of the central characters in this story is the mutant named Angel. Flying high above the clouds on white wings that emerge from his back, which resemble those of a dove, Angel gives explicit voice to Gaiman's argument. While nonmutants connect through the orthodox bonds of "country and creed," through Angel's thoughts, Gaiman reveals that mutants are joined by their "strangeness" (Gaiman et al. 2003, 132).

To understand how the subjugation of women informs Gaiman's work, I draw heavily from Silvia Federici (2012), who chronicles the witch hunts from the past and the ways male authority has been legislated as part of the social order to demonize women. In *Marvel 1602*, we have a creative exploration of how patriarchy is accomplished through a policing of difference and strangeness. We are offered a vivid reminder of the horrors done to the innocent. We also see a group of very uncanny individuals uniting to challenge the dominant social order by embracing their marginalized and dispossessed status as witchbreed.

A fictional story can never truly grasp or bear witness to the atrocities visited on those who were accused of witchcraft, tortured, and killed. But there is value in remembering the pain and trauma that emerge from toxic prejudices as well as imagining a space where abject individuals can come together in interesting ways to confront persecution and attempt to build a new and different kind of world. Gaiman's recrafting of the story of the X-Men traces the way he understands persecution and introduces the idea of a new kind of solidarity as a response to injustice. The eloquent Ursula Le Guin (2007) wrote, "The literature of imagination, even when tragic, is reassuring, not necessarily in the sense of offering nostalgic comfort, but because it offers a world large enough to contain alternatives, and therefore offers hope" (87). It is with this guiding idea that I acknowledge the inability of a fantasy text to capture and reproduce an historic event while simultaneously taking hope in the power of fiction to reveal to readers how toxicity is

accomplished, as well as some of the ways it might be challenged and overcome.

WITCH HUNTS

Marvel 1602 includes a large cast of characters pulled from popular Marvel
comics. Famous characters such as Thor and Captain America appear in
Marvel 1602, and the audience is also introduced to Peter Parker who has not
yet been bitten by a radioactive spider. My work focuses narrowly on the
portion of the story dealing with Gaiman's imagination of the X-Men, particularly the use of mutants as witchbreed. In the original X-Men comics, the
team is led by Professor Charles Xavier, a telepath who can read the thoughts
of others and control their minds. The rest of the original team includes Scott
Summers (Cyclops), Jean Grey (Marvel Girl/Phoenix), Bobby Drake (Iceman), Hank McCoy (Beast), and Warren Worthington (Angel). Each has
incredible mutant powers that set them apart from the rest of humanity. Three
important villains from the original comics also appear: Erik Lensherr (Magneto), Wanda Maximoff (Scarlet Witch), and Pietro Maximoff (Quicksilver).
In *Marvel 1602*, the cast is reimagined and renamed: Carlos Javier leads a
team of mutants with Journeyman Scotius Summerisle, Apprentice John
Grey (a disguised Jean), Journeyman Roberto Trefusis, Master Hal McCoy,
and Apprentice Werner. The villains appear as Enrique (the Grand Inquisitor) along with Petros and Sister Wanda. Carlos Javier describes his team of
mutants as *omnia mutantur*, which translates as everything changes. While
Javier calls his students mutantur, those who serve the Inquisition use the
disparaging term witchbreed to refer to what the traditional Marvel Universe
refers to as mutants.

Early in the narrative, we meet Werner (Angel), who is captured by the
soldiers of the Inquisition and sentenced to be burned at the stake. Werner's
thoughts and memories are revealed in the comic book panels. He knows a
Jew was burned the day before as a heretic. Gaiman does not soften the
imagery. Instead, the reader is told in stark words what happened, "A stench
of woodsmoke and burning hair, then a smell of meat cooking. There were
screams" (Gaiman 2003, 6). Imprisoned with death waiting, Werner laments
that he will never fly again. Meanwhile, the Grand Inquisitor meets with
Petros (Quicksilver), who reports of his meeting with James the VI, the next
in line for the throne of England. Petros tells the Grand Inquisitor that James
is amendable to an alliance because there is "common cause against [. . .]
witches, magicians, and witchbreed, who infest England like lice crawling
through a shepherd's crotch" (Gaiman et al. 2003, 20). The discourse of
scapegoating is made intelligible through the dehumanizing reference to
witchbreed as parasites who infest the country.

To justify the torture of witchbreed and their planned extermination, Gaiman (2003) demonstrates how the mutants are seen as monsters that are less than human. Historically, monsters are beings of such malignant evil that they threaten to destroy entire communities (Cummings and Stanescu 2007, 65). They appear in discourse as representations of our worst fears, and at the appearance of the monster, the duty of the sovereign becomes parallel to the duty of a shepherd to the flock: they must protect the community at any cost from the violence and damage the monster brings (Macke and Cummings 2009, 52). A monster cannot be reasoned with. It can only be destroyed. The maternal monster is especially fearsome, which is evident from early classical examples such as Grendel's mother in the poem *Beowulf* to contemporary science-fiction films such as the *Alien* series. Often the feminine monster within mythology is tied to a divide between the rhetorical figure of the nurturing mother and the devouring mother (Rushing 1989, 6). With the figure of the witch, we have the epitome of the devouring mother. The alliance between James the VI and the Inquisition in *Marvel 1602* is built on a fiction that imagines witchbreed as monsters that must be destroyed at any cost. Once a group of individuals is rhetorically framed as an invading pest, the logic of extermination becomes a viable and reasonable response.

Gaiman's presentation of the mutants as less than human is continued and echoed in the words of the Grand Inquisitor. At one point he even remarks, "Perhaps I should order them to daub his [Werner's] wings with pitch, or wax, so the damned creature will burn like a *torch* for *righteousness*" (Gaiman 2003, 21). Notice that Werner is no longer a human being who is punished for doing wrong. Instead, he is decried as a damned creature. The dehumanizing labeling of witchbreed is made even more explicit in the conversation between the Grand Inquisitor and Werner that follows:

Grand Inquisitor: It is almost *dawn*, monster. Are you prepared to repent your *heresies*, before you reach the cleansing fire?

Werner: I am no *monster*. I am as my creator *made* me.

Grand Inquisitor: You counterfeit an *angel*, aye. But your creator is the *Devil*. (Gaiman 2003, 28)

Werner is named as a monster and, although he defends himself, that line of defense is rejected by the Grand Inquisitor. The reader sees the fear in Werner's eyes as a torch is brought forward to light the fire in order to burn him alive at the stake.

The Grand Inquisitor's fear of the mutant as well as his assertion that he is the creation of the devil is represented throughout Western culture. The parallels to the witch hunts of the past are clear. No doubt, as Gaiman develops his argument about the persecution of witchbreed, it is useful to revisit the persecution of witches in what is one of the most virulent and toxic moments in the long history of patriarchal violence. Witches in fairy tales are the stuff of nightmares. From early childhood, I was told stories of witches where the usual refrain was that they eat the hearts of children and use evil magic to impose the devil's will on unsuspecting victims. Some of the older stories come from ancient mythology where witches such as Circe used magic to turn men into swine and where Morgana Le Fey drew upon demonic power to try to destroy Camelot. Other fairy tales, such as Hansel and Gretel and Snow White, include witches who are malevolent beings and true incarnations of evil. Learning about the witches of fantasy and those who were and are being accused today of witchcraft is imperative. Put simply, fairy tales reveal inner struggles and help society consider collective solutions to problems (Bettelheim 2010, 5).

The witches of the Western collective imagination are monstrous, and *Marvel 1602* provides a lens for us to see that the mutants in Gaiman's narrative are viewed as equally monstrous. However, we know that the mutants—who represent the real individuals who were historically accused of witchcraft and punished as witches—are guilty only of being different. To make the impact and connection obvious, it is worth noting that those persecuted during the witch hunts were victims of pernicious propaganda and a moral panic that resulted in hundreds of thousands of deaths (De Blécourt 2000, 288–89). Gender was clearly an important variable, although other factors figured prominently. Part of making sense of the violence perpetrated during the witch hunts requires us to explore the animus that was so easily spread against those accused of witchcraft just because their gender, identity, or performance were different.

Silvia Federici (2012) offers a compelling thesis on the cause of the persecution of witches that utilizes a lens incorporating gender, race, and class. Rather than isolating just one part of the social fabric, she delves deeply into the ways several factors coalesced together. Her work is especially interested in the power constellation that created the necessary conditions for the possibility of witch hunts to occur in the first place. She writes,

> Women were terrorized through fantastic accusations, horrendous torture, and public executions because their social power had to be destroyed—social power that in the eyes of their persecutors was obviously significant, even in the case of older women. Old women, in fact, carried the collective memory of the community. (Federici 2012, 13)

In exploring the various kinds of labor that women performed, one readily notices that many of the women who historically worked as midwives, medics, and sex workers were the very ones who ended up accused of witchcraft

(Federici 1988, 46). As such, women found themselves in positions of resistance to the dominant orders of science, religion, and patriarchal systems of governance. They found themselves in competition with powerful individuals at a time when communities desired a person to punish for everything from a bad year of crops to the tragic loss of a child. The sexual dimension is important to how Federici (2018) formulates her argument. Where women previously had a much greater degree of sexual freedom and control over their own bodies and reproduction, the new regime demanded that they be submissive and subservient. Federici (2018) explains this, noting, "Thus, no effort was spared to paint female sexuality as something dangerous for men and to humiliate women in such a way as to curb their desire to use their bodies to attract them. Never in history have women been subjected to such a massive, internationally organized, legally approved, religiously blessed assault on their bodies" (31).

The interrelationship between this assault on women's bodies and the institution of a new regime of control over women's labor is important for understanding how social reproduction functioned during this time. Anne Barstow (1994) advances the argument that there was significant overlap between the treatment of women and the treatment of other unfree persons during this time period, writing,

> A closer look reveals that, in fact, free women and slaves of both sexes fell into many of the same categories in the eyes of early modern European men. Neither had control over what they produced, other than in exceptional circumstances, and their labor could be coerced. Both were seen by the law as children, as fictive minors who could be represented in court only by their masters/husbands. Both could be legally beaten, debased, and humiliated. When mistreated, both were impotent to gain help from others within their group, nor usually could their families help them. (159–60)

Barstow (1994) contends that the treatment of witches as subhuman opened opportunities for an exceptional form of marginalization where their economic and social status could be controlled, thereby solidifying the power of men to behave in even more authoritarian and paternalistic ways.

In *Marvel 1602,* Gaiman connects his reimagining of historical witch hunts to both sovereign and ecclesiastical authority. Just as the witch hunts of the past required coordination between the church and the state so too does the hunting of witchbreed in Gaiman's tale. The Grand Inquisitor, Petros, and Sister Wanda are positioned in Spain during the Inquisition. However, the Grand Inquisitor dispatches Petros, who is gifted with the mutant ability to run at near blinding speeds, to communicate with James the VI, who will be the future king of England. Petros arrives and notifies James the VI that the Grand Inquisitor is willing to continue his campaign against the witchbreed in exchange for the promise that when Carlos Javier and his students are taken, they will be turned over to him. These terms are agreed to and an alliance between the Grand Inquisitor and the Protestant future king is made.

The intrigue deepens when a messenger from the Pope arrives to confront the Grand Inquisitor about his secret dealings with James the VI. As the messenger and the Grand Inquisitor descend into the subterranean caverns beneath the fortress of the Inquisition, they speak privately about concerns that his Holiness the Pope has about the Grand Inquistitor's actions. The messenger reveals that he is tasked with killing the Grand Inquisitor in a way that will make it appear as an accident. Drawing a blade of Toledo steel, he moves to complete the assassination. But steel is no danger to the master of magnetism. At this moment his nonchalant demeanor as he floats and reverses the blade to kill the messenger, divulges to the reader that the Grand Inquisitor is really the mutant Magneto.

In discussing the causes of witch hunts, Federici (2004) argues that the subjugation of women that occurred was connected not only to religious and political power but also ultimately to the economic structures of capital. She maintains that the hunting of witches was part of an extraction of wealth from the commons to the elites. If we consider the historical context in which the witch hunts occurred, the gender and class of the accused, and the effects of the persecution, then we must conclude that witch hunting in Europe was an attack on women's resistance to the spread of capitalist relations, as well as the power that women had gained over their sexuality, control of reproduction, and their ability to heal. Witch hunting was also instrumental to the construction of a new patriarchal order where women's bodies, their labor, as well as their sexual and reproductive powers were placed under control of the state and transformed into economic resources (Federici 2004, 170).

Federici (2004) ties the extraction of labor from the masses to Karl Marx (1885) and his work on primitive accumulation. Marx (1885) maintains that the ways massive wealth is accumulated is due to the unequal use of force by the wealthy to exploit the weak. The powerful ensnare the weak and coerce them into uneven labor relations. Marx contrasts this explanation with the one offered in the work of Adam Smith (1776), who suggested that wealth accumulates from industrious and intelligent workers who save the capital from their labor. The result is two competing stories for the acquisition of wealth. In the capitalist narrative, bright and industrious individuals amass great wealth from their talent and sweat. They then use that wealth to build businesses and investments, which increases their status in society because of how well they have leveraged their exceptional work into greater wealth and influence. The poor, in contrast, are perceived to be less capable, less talented, and less hard working. The competing narrative offered by Marx (1885) finds this explanation lacking and suggests instead that the wealthy generally are those who prey upon the poor and extract wealth from others. In mining the labor of the proletariat, the powerful amass vast wealth while keeping their hands on the levers of power so that any challenge to their authority is easily contained. For Marx (1885), poverty is not the result of being lazy or stupid. Instead, it occurs because the powerful have seized the means of production and exploit the poor to amass greater wealth for themselves in which to position themselves as the elite.

This interpretation of wealth is particularly useful to Federici (2004) who, while acknowledging the need for a more thorough understanding of colonialism, nevertheless uses the theory of primitive accumulation to conclude that the violent shift from feudal societies to capitalism was marked by a brutal redefinition of the role of women in society (62–63). Central to her thesis is the idea that coercive labor required the taming and subjugation of women and that occurred through the torture and killing of witches. To build a capitalist economy required a huge number of laborers who could be paid cheaply to do what was often dangerous work. This required a paradigmatic shift where opposition to the newly emerging order was crushed.

The witch hunts of Europe were brought to the New World and, while many are familiar with the Salem Witch Trials, the Inquisition also conducted hunts in Latin America (Pavlac 2009, 158). Federici (2004) notes that in order to divest people from their land and wealth, an alibi was needed to provide some measure of cover. Identifying native people as "cannibals, devil-worshippers, and sodomites" provided an alternative explanation for what could then be categorized as a religious mission, when in fact the purpose was clearly "conquest" (Federici 2004, 221). In short, the expansion of gendered violence transitioned into other forms of colonial violence in order to consolidate wealth.

Gaiman's story also connects to the question of colonialism with sovereign violence. Gaiman connects the persecution of the witchbree d to marginalized groups and the policing of difference. As the story progresses, Queen Elizabeth the I dies, and James the VI of Scotland becomes James the I of England. At this point, the Grand Inquisitor is betrayed by a fellow mutant, Toad, who is highly placed within the Vatican. Toad reveals that Enrique is witchbreed. The capture of Enrique, Sister Wanda, and Petros follows and all are sentenced to be burned at the stake. The reader is offered more insight into what motivates Enrique when he is confronted by a church official who speaks with him directly before he is to be burned:

> You were born a Jew, in the Ghetto of Venice. When you were five years old, you strayed from the Ghetto. You were . . . detained, and baptized, by an overenthusiastic priest, who took a liking to you. You must have been a pretty child, for a Jew. When the Jews begged for you to be returned, the Holy Father explained that, while he was sorry, he would not imperil your immortal soul. He explained that it was *unfortunate*, but returning a baptized child to the Christ-killers would doom you to hell. (Gaiman 2003, 155)

Enrique's response confirms the disdain he holds for human beings and for the church he served, "I was taught all I needed to know about your kind, when I was a weeping child, pleading to be allowed back to my people and my family" (Gaiman 2003, 156).

The reasoning and apparent motives of the church official in Gaiman's narrative mirror Federici's (2004) thesis that the witch hunts were largely about usurping authority from those who, because of race, gender, class, or faith, existed outside the dominant capitalist order. Of course, while gender is rarely the singular explanation, Pavlac (2009) writes,

> Nevertheless, the numbers of female victims, the sexualized methods of perse-cution, and the many misogynist foundational ideas all signify a notable fe-male dimension to the witch hunts. The specifics of the hunts grew out of Western Society's long tradition of female subordination. Laws and customs show how women were valued less than men. In practical terms, this devalua-tion included paying women less, restricting their control of wealth and prop-erty, and forbidding access to many professions. (194)

The move to dehumanize women and others who pose a threat to the emerg-ing apparatus of the capitalist state relied upon a toxic logic that allowed strict control over sexuality, reproduction, and labor.

The violence of patriarchy is visible in specific destructive modes of toxic masculinity. The primary forms of toxic masculinity include misogyny, homophobia, greed, and violent domination (Kupers 2005, 716). Isolated examples of individual behavior appear throughout *Marvel 1602* that fit within this definition. Scotius Summerisle (Cyclops) becomes territorial with Werner when he perceives that Werner is romantically interested in John Grey. That escalates into a jealous rage until the moment he realizes that Werner does not know that John is Jean. The behavior of James the VI also reflects hypermasculinity in his predatory advances toward young Petros, who he clearly wants to groom as his sexual partner.

At the macrolevel, the toxicity is more readily apparent. In fact, wounded masculinity often appears in cultural texts in a way that presents itself as a crisis to hegemonic forms of masculinity (Johnson 2017a, 23). This is situat-ed in individuals. However, it also occurs in broader political anxieties where fragile masculinity is defined in relation to an imagined threat. No doubt, the current political milieu in the United States demonstrates that Donald Trump's efficacy as a rhetorical leader is tied to his demagoguery around the creation and maintenance of a political subject that feels slighted by the imagined threats of those who might alter the perceived American way of life (Johnson 2017b, 241). With the history of the persecution of witches, there is a microlevel where individuals' misogyny, greed, homophobia, and violent domination are perceptible. However, the toxicity also rises to the level of being transparent in the broader culture and politics through the management of social relations at the macrolevel.

Discovering how the toxic prejudices of the past inform contemporary iterations of violence is difficult. But certainly there is an intersection between misogyny, racism, and colonialism that was at play in the treatment of witches that continues to be refined and, in many ways, defines politics and culture today. The witch hunts of the past are dressed today in new clothing, but they are an eerie and familiar refrain of what came before. In analyzing how violence occurs today, Jim Burns (2017) writes, "The carefully cultivated belief in America's exceptional status and ostensive moral superiority in and over the world has rationalized and justified settler-colonial genocide, slavery, lynching, sexual and gender violence, economic deprivation, and drone wars—truly a biopolitical history that starkly illustrates the power and willingness to kill and let die" (180). There is no need for a leap of faith to connect the mature modes of violence occurring today to the discursive and material modes of subjugation that paved the way for their emergence. In *Marvel 1602,* the demonization of the witchbreed is tied to a desire to exterminate difference in order to preserve a notion of a particular kind of humanity at risk. Humans are presented as fragile and vulnerable in order to justify violence against outsiders. This replicates the logic of extermination used in the witch hunts of the past through a mode of threat construction, which continues to define the current American political constellation.

The haunting figure of the witch does interesting work in *Marvel 1602*. She is a potent reminder of how darker impulses led humanity to a moral panic where thousands were killed. Disciplinary tactics used to police the bodies of mutants in *Marvel 1602* echo and retell the story of violence done to so many. However, Gaiman's reimagining of the witch hunts also provides the reader with a toolkit to organize resistance. An analysis of how the mutants contested the suppression of the witch hunts is instructional in considering how such forces have been and can be resisted in our own time.

SEASON OF THE WITCH

Moments before the execution of Werner (Angel), Scotius Summerisle (Cyclops) and Roberto Trefusis (Iceman) arrive and stage a rescue. Roberto freezes the torch and shoots a sheet of ice at the guards, while Scotius uses an optic blast to break the chains holding Werner. The mutantur escape and together set sail from Spain toward the coast of England. Werner is introduced to the apprentice John Grey (a disguised Jean Grey), who is using her powers of telekinesis to propel the ship. Scotius reveals a jagged red X, branded on the left side of his chest over his heart, as he changes his shirt. He remarks, "They *brand* monsters, where I come from, before they *drown* them" (Gaiman 2003, 35). The repeated refrain of labeling witchbreed as monsters reinforces how language is used to construct mutantur as enemies. The interesting subtext here is perhaps to share the idea for how this group might come to be known as the X-Men.

It is useful to briefly turn from the narrative and consider the contrast between the leadership style of Carlos Javier (Professor X) and the Grand Inquisitor (Magneto). In the original X-Men comics, Magneto is a sympathetic if misguided villain. He is a Holocaust survivor who genuinely believes that the persecution of mutants precedes an inevitable war between homo sapiens (humans) and homo superior (mutants). In several story arcs, Magneto joins and even leads the X-Men as anti-mutant sentiment intensifies and mutants are called to register and to live in camps. An example of this is the graphic novel *God Loves, Man Kills*. This novel tells a story where a group of purifiers hunt and kill mutants. The dead bodies of the slain are hung publicly with the sign "Die Mutie" attached to the corpses. Magneto joins the X-Men in battle against the purifiers and the evangelical minister who leads them (Claremont 1994). In two interviews, Chris Claremont explains that the leadership styles of Professor X and Magneto are in some ways analogous to the contrast between Martin Luther King and Malcolm X (Hanks 2011; Bekris 2015). Like King, Professor X believes in the possibility of a world of peaceful coexistence between humans and mutants. In contrast, Magneto is militant and pro-mutant in a way that echoes the approach of Malcom X.

While this interpretation of the roles of Professor X and Magneto has some support, there is also some dissent (Shyminsky 2006). And, while Magneto is occasionally presented as an ally to the X-Men, he is also usually represented as a zealot who is so enamored by his beliefs that he is willing to make morally dubious sacrifices for the cause. Chris Claremont shared in an interview that he intended a comparison for Magneto to Menachim Begin since Magneto also starts his life as a terrorist and then redeems himself (Bekris 2015). Gaiman captures some of the tension in Magneto's motivations. As the Grand Inquisitor, Magneto clearly has a plan to gain power and advance his own agenda. He burns those mutants who cannot pass as human at the stake to solidify his authority as Grand Inquisitor. Meanwhile, he secrets away many mutants to a hidden location in preparation for the eventual conflict with humanity. But along the way, we discover that his friendship with Carlos Javier exists despite their difference in methods, and that he has a genuine desire to overthrow the institutions and people who are killing mutants.

The difference in the approach of Javier and Magneto on the question of how to interact with the surrounding world is important to how resistance is organized today. Magneto is presented by Gaiman as a militant isolationist. He argues for a future where mutants live separately from other humans.

Javier is much more inclusive. His vision builds upon the idea of an intersectional alliance between all of the various factions who oppose colonial violence. The separatism of Magneto is paired with a belief that the ends justify the means, while the idealism of Carlos Javier is premised on the idea of an intersectional resistance to structures of domination. Magneto wants nothing to do with humans and sees them as problematic allies, while Javier wants an ethics of cohabitation where all live together peacefully.

The question of how different prejudices interact is the subject of much ongoing discussion. Kimberle Crenshaw (1989) opened part of this dialogue with her pioneering work on the subject of intersectionality—a term she uses to explain how antiracist strategies must take into account both sexism and patriarchy. Crenshaw's (1989) legal analysis highlights the challenges black women face because their oppression occurs at the intersection of their status as both women and people of color. The combination of racism and sexism makes the violence and discrimination done to women of color a different kind of problem than either racism or sexism in isolation. Crenshaw explains (1989),

> This focus on the most privileged group members marginalizes those who are multiply-burdened and obscures claims that cannot be understood as resulting from discrete sources of discrimination. I suggest further that this focus on otherwise-privileged group members creates a distorted analysis of racism and sexism because the operative conceptions of race and sex become grounded in experiences that actually represent only a subset of a much more complex phenomenon. (140)

Crenshaw (1989) advances the case that dealing with racism and sexism should involve addressing the problems of the most disadvantaged. Part of what makes Crenshaw's (1989) analysis so groundbreaking is that she correctly diagnoses the ways patriarchy amplifies racism and vice versa. The root of the problem is rarely just one form of oppression. Part of the explanation for how Magneto ends up as the Grand Inquisitor is that he was torn from his family as a child because he was Jewish. If oppression is intersectional, then one possible way to contest the various intersections of subjugation might be for outcasts and misfits to ally together to oppose any persecution that originates in the demonization of those who are different, regardless if it's by race, gender, class, or personhood.

Gaiman's gambit for revealing the differences in leadership becomes most explicit as the narrative of the witchbreed mutants moves to the conclusion. The planned execution of the three witchbreed (Enrique/Magneto, Petros, and Wanda) is halted when Magneto uses his powers to break free from the chains. With the help of Petros and Wanda, Magneto quickly dispatches the guards and soldiers. They then set sail for the coast of Newfoundland to rejoin the many mutants who could pass as human that Magneto has secreted away. Gaiman does not provide insight into why his Magneto only aimed to save those witchbreed who could pass. Furthermore, his Magneto is a marked departure from the Magneto in other X-Men stories who sees beauty in being different and who finds human definitions of what is normal, beautiful, ugly, inadequate, and antiquated. The rationale for killing those who could not pass seems to be a calculation on his part to make any necessary sacrifices to best optimize his chance for victory. Magneto's ship does not sail to the Newfoundland. Instead, it is drawn to the ship piloted by Jean Grey, with the assistance of Carlos Javier. Joined by various other heroes of the Marvel Universe, the mutantur arrive in Roanoke, Virginia, where they declare independence from England and initiate the founding of a new independent country. Together, the heroes learn that the temporal break that sent Rojhaz (Captain America) back will destroy all existence. To repair the temporal distortion, Magneto teams up with Thor to produce galvanic energy to channel lightning and mend the break. This causes the multiverse of Marvel universes to be saved, while the universe of *Marvel 1602* is brought to an end.

The narrative at this point becomes weird for those not familiar with the group of individuals in the Marvel Universe known as the Watchers. For those not deeply steeped in the lore of the Marvel multiverse, what follows will seem like a strange deus ex machina. A Watcher is a powerful being that observes and witnesses the universe as it unfolds (Fleming 2008). In *Marvel 1602*, Uatu is the Watcher who has been a witness to the events as they have transpired. After the distortion is repaired, he notices that time is healed and that all will be as it was supposed to—with the age of heroes happening much later. The council he serves then makes the decision that the universe of *Marvel 1602* can continue as a tiny universe held and carried by Uatu. When he peers down at the little universe, the reader sees the new world that is emerging. Instead of being destroyed, the survivors have gathered together. The role of the Watcher in the *Marvel 1602* narrative is useful in explaining why the entire multiverse has been saved by the heroes of this small universe, but also how the characters will continue to exist in a parallel space to the regular Marvel heroes of present time. Basically, this side story allows for an explanation of how the heroes of *Marvel 1602* have saved the cosmos while also providing a basis for how future stories in the universe of *Marvel 1602* are possible.

In the aftermath, Enrique speaks again with Carlos Javier. Having saved the universe, he is owed a boon and he tells Carlos that he and the many mutantur he saved are to be left alone, and that Carlos is to keep Wanda and Petros, Enrique's children, and teach them. While Magneto has been essential to saving this Marvel Universe, he remains a troubling figure who is willing to use and sacrifice others as pawns to accomplish his goals. Because Magneto uses others as instruments, his approach is easy to critique. The cultural question of separatism is much more complicated. It is a question that emerges in a variety of hero narratives. For example, the people of Wakanda and their leader, Black Panther, also grapple with whether they should interact with the world around them or live apart. While Gaiman does not offer a strong defense for the benefits of separatism, he does devote significant rhetorical energy to the argument for an alliance among outcasts.

AN ANTHEM FOR OUTCASTS

The combination of patriarchy, colonialism, and capitalism are incredibly toxic. Sadly, creating strategies to resist these interlocking oppressions is challenging. It is useful to recall LeGuin's (2007) defense of fantasy and imagination as resources for discovering ways of thinking and being different. *Marvel 1602* does not propose a simple solution to the carnage brought about by toxic prejudices. But it does suggest that there is strength in numbers and that those who are persecuted can align with allies to avoid being isolated and eliminated. Federici argues in an interview that we need new rhetorical representations that challenge toxicity, stating,

> The continuity of the forms of persecution and oppression deployed against women is evident in cinema and television. Degrading images of women have persisted in cinematic representations and such images continue to contribute to a culture dominated by the fear of women, a culture in which the woman is a witch, aggressive, lustful, obsessively committed to revenge, possessed with inextinguishable hatreds. We need healing images and images of resistance. (Austin 2018)

Marvel 1602 is a potential example for those who are different on how we might imagine ourselves uniting together to challenge injustice. Mutantur are persecuted and hunted because they are dangerous. When they join together, they form a community with the strength, resources, and abilities to defend themselves. Scott Bukatman (1994) writes, "The group is something more than a battle unit and clearly takes the form of an idealized, alternative society—one in which all members, and therefore no members are outcasts" (73).

In reading stories of witches and witch hunts, one common thread mentioned in each of the works on witches cited in this essay is that those who were targeted frequently were older women who did not have families or the social relations sufficient to deter those who would condemn them. The most vulnerable members of society were the easiest to bring charges against. It seems counterintuitive to believe that the most precarious of those who live among us would be perceived as being such an incredible threat to the apparatus of control that there would be a need for them to be publicly executed.

And we should remember why the publicity of the punishment is so important. It is a method of domination that exhibits control over unruly subjects. The ways that a contagion of fear is spread is by showing a tortured and mutilated body so that others will be cowed. It is not at all farfetched to argue that the witch hunts were made possible by a hideous kind of bullying in which individuals with little ability to resist were isolated, abused, and killed.

One message of *Marvel 1602* is that we who are strange and different are not alone. X-Men stories remind us that there are villains out there who will persecute outcasts. The forms of maltreatment range from registration and public shaming to torture and execution. We are also invited to think about how to respond to injustice. Perhaps the most admirable aspect to the approach offered by Carlos Javier is that we can build spaces in our society where those who are hunted can find sanctuary and where an ethic of peaceful coexistence can reign. What we need is a juridical system that treats injustice, violence, and abuse as deviant while simultaneously accepting the strangeness, singularity, and dignity of every individual. When the system we live in valorizes predatory behavior and allows the powerful to demonize and pathologize the weak, the moment to act becomes especially urgent. How will we respond when the most vulnerable among us find themselves at risk? Imagine if all of the outcasts of the world united together under the aegis of peace and justice to defend the vulnerable. It would truly signal the dawn of the age of heroes.

REFERENCES

Anczyk, Adam, and Joanna Malita-Król. 2017. "Women of Power: The Image of the Witch and Feminist Movements in Poland." *Pomegranate* 19, no. 2.

Austin, Arlen, Beth Capper, and Rebecca Schneider. 2018. "Times of Dispossession and (Re)-Possession: An Interview with Silvia Federici." *TDR/The Drama Review* 62, no. 1, 131–42.

Barstow, Anne Llewellyn. 1994. *Witchcraze: A New History of the European Witch Hunts.* Harper Collins.

Bekris, Niko. 2015. "Interview with Chris Claremont Part 1." ChristComicsCoffee.com https://christcoffeecomics.com/2015/06/24/interview-with-chris-claremont-part-1/.

Bettelheim, Bruno. 2010. *The Uses of Enchantment: The Meaning and Importance of Fairy Tales.* New York: Vintage Books.

Bukatman, Scott. 1994. "X-Bodies: The Torment of the Mutant Superhero." *Uncontrollable Bodies: Testimonies of Identity and Culture*, 92–129.

Burns, Jim. 2017. "Biopolitics, Toxic Masculinities, Disavowed Histories, and Youth Radicalization." *Peace Review* 29, no. 2, 176–83.

Claremont, Chris, Brent Eric Anderson, and Steve Oliff. 1994. *X-Men: God Loves, Man Kills.* Marvel Comics.

Crenshaw, Kimberle. 1989. "Demarginalizing the Intersection of Race and Sex: A Black Feminist Critique of Antidiscrimination Doctrine, Feminist Theory and Antiracist Politics." *U. Chicago Legal Forum.*

Cummings and Stanescu. 2007. "Argumentation and Democratic Disagreement: On Cultivating a Practice of Dissent." *Controversia* 5:2, Summer 2007: 55-76.

Darowski, Joseph J. 2014. *X-Men and the Mutant Metaphor: Race and Gender in the Comic Books.* Lanham, MD: Rowman & Littlefield.

De Blécourt, Willem. 2000. "The Making of the Female Witch: Reflections on Witchcraft and Gender in the Early Modern Period." *Gender & History* 12, no. 2, 287–309.

Federici, Silvia. 2018. *Witches, Witch-Hunting, and Women*. PM Press.

———. 2012. *Revolution at Point Zero: Housework, Reproduction, and Feminist Struggle*. London: PM Press.

———. 2004. *Caliban and the Witch: Women, the Body, and Primitive Accumulation*. Brooklyn, NY: Autonomedia.

———. 1988. "The Great Witch-Hunt." *The Maine Scholar*, 1, 31–52.

Fleming, James R. 2008. "Incommensurable Ontologies and the Return of the Witness in Neil Gaiman's 1602." *ImageTexT: Interdisciplinary Comics Studies* 4, no. 1.

Gaiman, Neil, Andy Kubert, Richard Isanove, Todd Klein, Scott McKowen, and Steve Ditko. 2003. *Marvel 1602*. Marvel Comics.

Hanks, Henry. 2011. "The Secret to 'X-Men's' Success." CNN.com http://www.cnn.com/2011/SHOWBIZ/Movies/06/03/xmen.legacy.go/index.html.

Johnson, Paul Elliott. 2017a."Walter White(ness) Lashes Out: Breaking Bad and Male Victimage." *Critical Studies in Media Communication* 34, no. 1, 14–28.

———. 2017b. "The Art of Masculine Victimhood: Donald Trump's Demagoguery." *Women's Studies in Communication* 40, no. 3, 229–50.

Kupers, Terry A. 2005. "Toxic Masculinity as a Barrier to Mental Health Treatment in Prison." *Journal of Clinical Psychology* 61, no. 6, 713–24.

Lee, Stan, and Jack Kirby. 1963. "The X-Men #1." Marvel Comics.

Le Guin, Ursula K. 2007. "The Critics, the Monsters, and the Fantasists." *The Wordsworth Circle* 38, no. 1/2, 83–87.

Macke, Frank, and Kevin Cummings. 2009. "The Sign of the Monster." *Semiotics*, 501–12.

Marx, Karl. 1885 (1867). *Das Kapital: kritik der politischen ökonomie*. Germany: Verlag von Otto Meisner, 1894.

Pavlac, Brian A. 2009. *Witch Hunts in the Western World:Persecution and Punishment from the Inquisition through the Salem Trials*. ABC-CLIO.

Rushing, Jack. 2009. "Evolution of 'the new frontier' in *Alien and Aliens*: Patriarchal co-optation of the feminine archetype." *Quarterly Journal of Speech*, 75.2: 1-24.

Shyminsky, Neil. 2006. "Mutant Readers, Reading Mutants: Appropriation, Assimilation, and the X-Men." *International Journal of Comic Art* 8, no. 2, 387–405.

Smith, Adam. 1950. *An Inquiry into the Nature and Causes of the Wealth of Nations* (1776). Methuen.

Chapter Four

The Joker's Dionysian Philosophy of Gender and Sexuality in *The Dark Knight*

Jacob Murel

Throughout the years, Batman has undergone a series of reinterpretations. As Batman's creator Bob Kane once remarked, "every ten years Batman has to go through an evolution to keep up with the times" (Daniels 1999, 17). And, like Batman, so too has his equally famous archnemesis. Indeed, "the Joker has repeatedly morphed his mannerisms, appearance, and raison d'etre to meet the styles and trends of the time" (Hassoun 2015, 3). Every generation and cultural epoch gets its own Joker. The Joker of Tim Burton's *Batman* (1989) invoked the mob bosses of popular American mafia films released at the time while Cesar Romero's performance often seems like a conglomeration of the supporting villain and domestic comedy roles in which Romero partook throughout his career. But although scholars have had much to say on Batman's supposedly peculiar, and latent, sexuality—perhaps attributable to Fredric Wertham's (1954) infamous psychoanalysis of the character—academic scholarship has remained largely silent concerning the Joker's own sexuality and gender.

Given the continuing cultural prominence of Christopher Nolan's *The Dark Knight* (2008) and Heath Ledger's portrayal of the Joker therein, particularly their dual status as gold standards against which later performances are measured, this essay focuses on Heath Ledger's Joker in *The Dark Knight* as the central subject of the Joker's sexuality and gender. Frank Miller once described the Joker as "a homophobic nightmare" (Sharrett 1991, 36). Through a psychoanalytic reading of *The Dark Knight*, this essay aims to unpack this quote in reference to Heath Ledger's Joker while contextualizing him among other Joker variations in popular media. Ledger's Joker stands out as the most confrontational and sexually mercurial of Joker representa-tions in film and television. In demonstrating this, the present essay seeks to reveal, and thereby champion, the Joker's queerness against contemporary Western society's heterosexist norms.

To this end, the following essay regularly compares Ledger's Joker to other live-action versions of the Joker in both television and film. Drawing from previous scholarship on the 9/11 undertones throughout *The Dark Knight*, this essay argues that the Joker's critique of Gotham city's justice system and its incumbent moral code, which Batman represents and enforces, functions as a critique on conventional notions of individuated sexual iden-tities. In short, the Joker's cry for the abolishment of morality extends to gender and sexual identities. Through *The Dark Knight*'s psychoanalytic motifs, Ledger's Joker presents a mercurial sexuality and fluid gender iden-tity that disrupts traditional divisions such as homo/hetero and masculine/ feminine. This essay expands on this side of the Joker to show how his attack on Gotham City's state system can be likewise understood as an attempt to demolish categorized notions of gender and sexuality until the world, like himself, lives in pure, unindividuated sexuality.

Although many queer theorists debate the finer points of the term queer, Judith Halberstam (2005) offers a broad and functional definition of queer as meaning "nonnormative logics and organizations of community, sexual iden-tity, embodiment, and activity in space and time" (6). Most, if not every, past iteration of the Joker could fit beneath Halberstam's (2005) broad conceptual umbrella. For instance, Mario Rodriquez (2014) finds in Jack Nicholson's Joker a type of pimp. But he fails to mention how, in both attire and back-story, Nicholson reads like a carnivalesque spin on the mafia men from the 1970s and 1980s mobster films which immediately preceded the release of Tim Burton's *Batman*. His Joker is a mob boss motivated by lust and re-venge, focused primarily on winning (or rather, forcing) the affections of his former boss' lover Vicki Vale (Kim Bassinger). Earlier on, Caesar Romero portrayed the Joker as little more than a flamboyantly dressed rendition of the other villains Romero portrayed. Even ordinary humans like Batman's butler Alfred proved a challenge for the Joker, such as the season two epi-sode of the *Batman* television series, wherein Alfred outsmarts the Joker in laying a last-minute trap. Most recently, Jared Leto played the Joker in the 2016 *Suicide Squad* film, depicting him primarily as Harley Quinn's (Margot Robbie) abusive and controlling crime lord lover, obsessed only with freeing her from prison and reuniting them. The flamboyant attire and theatrical behavior of these Jokers invite Halberstam's (2005) concept of queer or nonnormative.

Compared to these previous iterations, however, Ledger's Joker in *The Dark Knight* is, quite simply, stranger as he seems more at home in a slasher film than a superhero summer blockbuster. While lust and revenge motivate

Nicholson's Joker, money drives Romero, and Leto is compelled by devotion to Harley Quinn; *The Dark Knight* offers no origin for the Joker nor explanation for his actions. He appears to kill without rhyme or reason. The film even promotes his lack of motivation. While Bruce Wayne (Christian Bale) attempts to discern the Joker's motives, his butler Alfred (Michael Cane) clarifies, "Some men aren't looking for anything logical, like money. They can't be bought, bullied, reasoned, or negotiated with. Some men just want to watch the world burn." The Joker is not a criminal in the traditional sense like Nicholson's performance, compelled by revenge, greed, or lust, but an unmotivated, chaotic force. In this sense, despite their appearance and theatrics, past Joker iterations are normative villains in that, for them, immorality and evil are means to some other end, be it a woman's affection or wealth. In turn, the Ledger Joker's contrasting lack of motivation means he operates on a nonnormative logic of villainy and violence, as though he were approaching them through Halberstam's (2005) definition of queer.

Alfred's statement, as with other features of the film, has been used by critics to establish a connection between Ledger's Joker and the representation of Middle Eastern terrorists in American media at the time of the film's release and interpret the film as a commentary or response to the national trauma of 9/11 (Baum 2009, 267–69; Muller 2011, 46–59; Nichols 2011, 236–50). Perhaps one of the clearest similarities between Ledger's Joker and contemporary terrorists is the Joker's low-quality camcorder videos of him torturing civilians broadcasted by the *Gotham City News*, echoing the infamous execution videos by terrorist organizations. The most overt instance of a Joker-terrorist connection is when Harvey Dent (Aaron Eckhart) asks the citizens of Gotham, in reference to the Joker, "Should we give in to this terrorist's demands?" Within this critical context, Alfred's remark stands out as an echo of President George W. Bush's address to Congress on September 20, 2001, wherein Bush claims that the terrorist organization Al-Qaeda's "goal is not making money; its goal is remaking the world" (Bush 2001). Here, Bush attributes to terrorist groups a transformative goal as described by Louise Richardson (2007), which "is not subject to negotiation, and its satisfaction would require the complete destruction of the regional state system" (13).

Theorists of gender and sexuality have long understood a connection between the state system and society's normative conceptualization of sexuality and gender. Nira Yuval-Davis (2008) explains how "constructed notions of nationhood usually involve specific notions of 'manhood' and 'womanhood'" (1). David Evans argues in *Sexual Citizenship: The Material Construction of Sexualities* (1993) that extant models of citizenship are rooted in patriarchal heterosexism. In volume 1 of *The History of Sexuality*, Michel Foucault (1978) similarly notes the late-capitalist development of biopower, which he understands as a form of social control enacted through the categorization of populations according to sexuality. Within all of these arguments is the idea of state systems tacitly producing and perpetuating rigid and demarcated categories for classifying gender and sexuality, as evidenced in state-based gender registries or the unmoving legislation regarding public restrooms organized by two genders.

In this critical context, the terrorist rhetoric surrounding Ledger's Joker reinforces his confrontational nonnormativity. In her article "Queer Times, Queer Assemblages," Jasbir Puar (2005) conceptualizes a "terrorist body [. . .] as a queer assemblage that resists queerness-as-sexual-identity" (121). She contrasts this notion of assemblage with the intersectionality often evoked in identity politics. She writes, "As opposed to an intersectional model of identity, which presumes components—race, class, gender, sexuality, nation, age, religion—are separable analytics and can be thus disassembled, an assemblage is more attuned to interwoven forces that merge and dissipate time, space, and body against linearity, coherency, and permanency" (Puar 2005, 127). In other words, the terrorist body as a queer assemblage opposes the very notion of a stable and demarcated identity, whether sexual or otherwise. This is because, as Puar (2005) clarifies in her summary of Achille Mdembe and Gayatri Spivak, the terrorist suicide-bomber, in turning the body into a weapon, blurs lines between metal and flesh, death of self and others, dying and becoming, as well as national or ideological sides. She writes,

> This dissolution of self into other/s and other/s into self not only effaces the absolute mark of self and other/s in the war on terror, it produces a systemic challenge to the entire order of Manichaean rationality that organizes the rubric of good versus evil. Delivering "a message inscribed on the body when no other means will get through," suicide bombers do not transcend or claim the rational or accept the demarcation of the irrational. Rather, they foreground the flawed temporal, spatial, and ontological presumptions on which such distinctions flourish. (Puar 2005, 130)

Here, the terrorist suicide-bomber acts as a queer assemblage disrupting normative and widely accepted divisions in society, such as those between self/other, rational/irrational, and good/evil. Puar (2005) includes sexual divisions here too, writing, "As a queer assemblage—distinct from the 'queering' of an entity or identity—race and sexuality are denaturalized through the impermanence, the transience of the suicide bomber; the fleeting identity replayed backward through its dissolution" (130). For Puar (2005), "terrorist bodies are nonheteronormative, if we consider nation and citizenship to be implicit in the privilege of heteronormativity, as we should" (131). But nonheteronormative here further means anti-individuation. The suicide bomber's attack on the state system functions as an attack on underlying notions of stable, even individuated, identity.

This interpretation of terrorist suicide bombers is important because, during one of the Joker's initial appearances in *The Dark Knight*, he acts as a suicide bomber. While proposing his plan of killing Batman to a collection of mob leaders, the Joker repeatedly insults them, provoking one mob leader to charge at the Joker. The Joker responds by revealing, and threatening to trigger, an assortment of grenades strapped to the inside of his trench coat. This threat of murder-by-suicide is merely a climatic disruption of the Joker's challenger to the entire order of Manichean rationality in which the mob leaders and Batman exist. In repeatedly denigrating the mob leaders, the Joker explains his plan to kill Batman in a way that alienates himself from both sides of Gotham's good/evil binary. Throughout this meeting, the mob leaders describe the Joker as a "two-bit whack-job," a "freak," and "crazy," yet he outsmarts the mob leaders at every rhetorical or intellectual turn during the meeting. In so doing, the Joker disrupts the mob leaders' conventional division between rational/irrational. The Joker's signature mode of murder further blurs conventional divisions of self/other in that he carves a Glasgow smile onto his victims and paints their faces to match his own, a grisly self-duplication that blurs boundaries between self/other and victim/victimizer. In this, the Joker's self-presentation as a suicide bomber signals his status as what Puar (2005) calls a queer assemblage disrupting the conventional divisions of a Manichean rationality.

The queer assemblage's disruption of fixed boundaries and stable identities is reinforced by the Ledger Joker's lack of origin or motivation. In remaining silent on the Joker's backstory, *The Dark Knight* presents a mercurial Joker. This comes to the fore throughout the film when the Joker continuously alters the origin of his facial scars to fit whomever he is talking with. This constantly shifting self-narrative disrupts the notion of a stable self. Eric Garneau (2015) notes in his overview of the various iterations of the Joker comics that the Joker's cultural success

> *thrives* on supposedly irreconcilable characterizations. [. . . T]he Joker depends on having a mutable identity, one full of "blurred borderlines" that ignore "chronology and sequence." Indeed it may be that Joker [. . . and his devotees] recognize something very important: that there is no such thing as fixed identity. (33–34)

This disruption of a stable identity extends to the Joker's gender and sexuality, particularly evidenced in his appearance.

In contrast to *The Dark Knight*'s conventionally masculine characters such as Bruce Wayne and Harvey Dent, the Joker evidences a more ambiguous sense of gender. Dressed in a purple and green suit, and engulfed by an oversized trench coat, the Joker evokes the psychotic serial killers typical of slasher films. In many renditions in film and comics of the Joker, his characteristic look is attributed to some form of genetic disfiguration. But throughout *The Dark Knight*, his characterizing makeup is smudged and smeared, revealing how Heath Ledger's Joker openly acts a part while removing all typical clothing that denotes physiological indicators of sex. His makeup, which "looks like the mask of death," dehumanizes his face, while his long, mangled hair and delimiting clothes render his body into a shapeless ambiguity (Zucker 1967, 308). He may be referenced by other characters with male pronouns, but he can visually pass as female. His chromatic restriction to white, green, and purple (shared by most Joker iterations) recalls the signifying tripartite color scheme donned by early twentieth-century American suffragettes of the Women's Social and Political Union (Crawford 1998, 136–37). In the end, he could just as easily be a woman, and his appearance would not change all that much in the film.

On this front, the 2011 three-part comic book series *Flashpoint: Batman, Knight of Vengeance* offers a prime example of the underlying gender ambiguity in Ledger's Joker. Set in an alternate universe, the *Flashpoint* comics depicts Batman fighting a female Joker. The Joker's sex, however, is never discussed outright, but eventually unveiled in a full-page panel at the end of the second installment. Particularly striking is the resemblance between this alternate reality's female Joker to Ledger's. Both have shoulder-length, green hair and a purple trench coat with similar vestments underneath. In addition, their shared facial disfiguration is the result of both makeup and oral scarring, the latter a motif first introduced in Ledger's performance. The resemblance seems especially important given the novelty of this Joker iteration. Traditionally, comics have portrayed the Joker as undeniably masculine in tailored suits and cropped hair, with Romero, Nicholson, and Leto all following suite. The resemblance between Ledger and this openly female Joker, particularly in light of this portrayal's novelty, emphasizes how a Joker of this appearance can believably create a visual ambiguous gender performance.

Meanwhile, the Joker's behavior smells of the sexual confusion typical of slasher film killers. It is next to impossible not to notice Joker's constant lip-licking in the film, being described by one critic as a "lip-smacking psychotic" (Hassoun 2015, 3). When considered alongside his preferred mode of killing—sticking a knife (and once, a grenade) into the mouth of his victim—the habit suggests a latent oral fixation. Sigmund Freud (1971a) conceived this fixation as "a weak point in the structure of the sexual function," resulting from a repressed infantile sexuality that persists in the unconscious (46). In this way, the Joker's oral fixation suggests that he is caught in psychosexual stasis, being "propelled by psychosexual fury, more particularly a male in gender distress" (Clover 2015, 77). Coupled with his lack of a coherent sense of gender or sexuality as suggested by his appearance, the Joker dons a symbolic sexual power to assert authority via his preferred primitive mode of killing, i.e., his phallic knife. During one of the only scenes in which the Joker actually wields a gun, upon being provoked by a mob boss, he immediately foregoes the gun and defects to his trademark knife as a means of asserting authority. Upon the Joker revealing this knife, the mob boss' henchmen switch allegiance and drag their former leader to his death. As with the slasher film killer described by Carol Clover (2015), the sexually distressed Joker employs the phallic object, here a knife, as a means of asserting (sexual) authority and power amid an ambiguous gender.

The Joker further employs knives as a means to intimacy. He explains, "Guns are too quick. You can't savor all the little emotions. You see, in their last moments, people show you who they really are." For the Joker, the physical proximity and emotional vulnerability involved in this primitive mode of murder produces a physical and emotional intimacy between killer and victim. During the film's two scenes in which the Joker is shown threatening someone with his knife, the Joker caresses the victim's face within inches of his own as he inserts the phallic knife into the victim's mouth. Meanwhile, the camera frame tightens and the background blurs as the Joker whispers how he received the scars forming his permanent smile with a different story to match the victim each time. Such intimate yet macabre encounters demonstrate how, for the Joker, "knives and needles, like teeth, beaks, fangs, and claws, are personal, extensions of the body that bring attacker and attacked into primitive, animalistic embrace" (Clover 2015, 81). So, when the Joker raids Harvey Dent's fundraiser, a knife protrudes from his shoe with which to attack Batman. Here, the knife becomes literalized as what it always was, an extension of the Joker's body and the means to a gruesome intimacy. It connects him both physically and emotionally with others while guarding him in a position of power.

Interestingly, throughout *The Dark Knight*, the Joker speaks of romance and sexuality in exclusively derisive terms. At Harvey Dent's fundraiser, the Joker espies Rachel (Maggie Gyllenhal) and laconically moans, "Hello, Beautiful," as he combs back his mangled hair. Later interrogated by Batman, the Joker teases his rival's evident crush on Rachel as he remarks between laughs, "Does Harvey know about you and his little bunny?" In both instances, the Joker openly mocks sexuality and romance despite performing his own erotic and intimate violence. In this regard, Heath Ledger's Joker is remarkably one-dimensional. Nicholson's Joker lusts after Vicki Vale, and Leto's Joker is driven by devotion to Harley Quinn. Even Romero's Joker is accompanied at times by his ruthless moll Queenie (Nancy Kovack), attempting in one episode to steal the S.S. *Gotham* ship at her behest. But throughout *The Dark Knight*, Ledger's Joker never deviates from his terrorism and erotic violence; he has no other characteristics—no pathos, no conventionally sexual behavior, nor even pleasure unrelated to violence. His delight rests only in intimate terror. Such flatness alongside his erotic violence suggests that, for the Joker, much like the archetypal slasher film killer, "violence and sex are not concomitants but alternatives, the one [. . .] a substitute and prelude to the other" (Williams 1992, 8). In other words, the Joker's psychosexual confusion leads to transferring his sexual energy and desires into erotic violence and theatrical horror. For this sexually disturbed Joker, violence replaces sex.

The Joker's replacement of sexuality with violence coincides with his traditional role as Batman's foil. Frank Miller describes Batman as "really the essence of sublimation," the result of Bruce Wayne sublimating his sexual impulses into the imposition of order through force and surveillance as Batman (Sharrett 1991, 37). Miller here evokes Freud's (1971b) theory of sublimation, which the latter understands as the transferring of sexual instincts into actions deemed to be of higher social value (79–80, 97). Rather than freely revel in the sexual liberties that naturally accompany his billionaire playboy lifestyle, Bruce Wayne abjures his sexual instincts to enforce order and justice as Batman, becoming, in the words of Police Commissioner Jim Gordon (Gary Oldman), "a silent protector, a watchful protector, a dark knight." Much as the Joker expresses his sexual instincts through violence and horror, Bruce Wayne sublimates his own sexual drive into the imposition of justice and order as Batman.

Batman's sublimation of sexuality into order generates the sort of Apollonian aura defined by Friedrich Nietzsche (2016), who writes, "it is the will of Apollo to bring rest and calm to individual beings precisely by drawing boundaries between them, and by reminding them constantly, with his demands for self-knowledge and measure, that these are the most sacred laws in the world" (50–51). For Nietzsche (2016), the Apollonian spirit brings structure, order, and morality. "As an ethical divinity Apollo demands measure from all who belong to him [. . .] whereas getting above oneself and excess were regarded as the true hostile demons of the non-Apolline sphere" (Nietzsche 2016, 27). As an enforcer of justice, Batman demands order from himself and others, refusing throughout the film to break his own moral code against killing. Though often chided by Alfred for neglecting to engage in any sexual or romantic relationships, Bruce Wayne demands both relentless self-knowledge and discipline from himself, sublimating his sexual impulses into the imposition of order and structure through Batman.

Importantly for Freud (1971b), sublimation only operates when instincts have been repressed by the societal demands of civilization, but the individual, still needing to satisfy these (sexual) instincts, deflects his/her sexual urges into "higher physical activities, scientific, artistic or ideological" (97). The general societal repression of sexual instincts serves as the prerequisite for Batman's sublimation. Similarly, the Joker's chaotic and erotic violence can be understood as a perverse erotic excess resulting from this same sexual repression. Robin Wood (1978) writes, "The release of sexuality in the horror film is always presented as perverted, monstrous, and excessive [. . .] both the perversion and the excess being the logical outcome of repression" (31–32). Resonant with figures like Norman Bates and Leatherface, which Wood (1978) offers to exemplify this perverted excess, the Ledger Joker's horrific yet erotic violence can be understood as a perverted and chaotic violence erupting from general societal repression of sexuality. While Bruce Wayne sublimates his sexual instincts to become an enforcer of society's order, the Joker's repressed and confused sexuality violently erupts as a chaotic excess disrupting that order.

In this, contrary to Batman's Apollonian order, the Joker's deflection of sexual drives into a chaotic terrorism and intimate violence recalls Nietzsche's (2016) reciprocal Dionysian impulse. In one scene from *The Dark Knight*, Batman interrogates the Joker inside a dim basement room at the Gotham City Police Department. They have the following interchange:

> JOKER: You have all these rules, and you think they'll save you.
> BATMAN: I have one rule.
> JOKER: Then that's the rule you'll have to break to know the truth.
> BATMAN: Which is?
> JOKER: The only sensible way to live in this world is without rules.

The Joker here argues against the sacred order Batman enforces. He argues, borrowing Nietzsche's (2016) terminology, "all the unmeasurable excess found in nature" (27). While Batman attempts to establish order and individuation through his sacred moral laws, the Joker advocates the complete abolishment of all order. His is "the attempt to cross the fixed boundaries of individuation [. . . as he regards] the state of individuation as the source and primal cause of all suffering, as something inherently to be rejected" (Nietzsche 2016, 50–52). The Joker's argument against rules and morality smells of the Dionysian philosophy as described by H. L. Mencken (2006) in his summary of Nietzsche's thought: "It is an argument for the actual facts of existence—however unrighteous and ugly those facts may be" (76).

While Batman sublimates his sexual desires into the imposition of a sacred order and morality, the Joker's repressed sexual instincts erupt as the disruption of that order, as chaotic excess. If Batman is divine order, the Joker is Dionysian chaos. Typical of the archetypal clown as described by Wolfgang Zucker (1967), the Joker revolts "against the confinement and definedness of the conditions into which [he] finds [him]self thrown" (308). In *The Dark Knight*, the Joker remarks, "Upset the established order, and everything becomes chaos. I'm an agent of chaos." Here, the Joker reveals himself as chaos itself in all its wild excess. While Batman represents an enforced order, the neat classification and division of life into defined structure, the Joker promulgates the reality of unindividuated being found in the

Dionysian spirit. He stands against society's neatly organized system of moral classifications, preferring instead to rest in pure being, living from nature and impulse in the world's natural amorality.

Though Batman seems to arise in response to the chaos and crime of Gotham City, the Joker's chaotic excess is equally produced by Batman's sacred order. During the aforementioned interrogation scene, the Joker tells Batman, speaking of Gotham's law-enforcing entities, "Their morals, their code, it's a bad joke. Dropped at the first sign of trouble. They're only as good as the world allows them to be. I'll show ya. When the chips are down, these . . . these civilized people, they'll eat each other." Here, again, the Joker argues for his Dionysian philosophy. As Jamey Heit (2011) aptly summarizes, the Joker claims that "the rational distinctions that uphold our cultural paradigms of good and evil are decidedly irrational in their false distinctions" (180). In other words, the Joker's actions are only considered evil inside of the arbitrariness of Batman's faux sacred moral order. The imposition of Batman's divine order produces the Joker's transgressive excess by sanctioning it as transgressive.

This critique of morality resonates with Judith Butler's (1990) critique of normative sexual practices, writing, "As a restriction of an originary fullness, the law prohibits some set of prepunitive sexual possibilities and the sanctioning of others. [. . . So] it would appear that the law produces *both* sanctioned heterosexuality and transgressive homosexuality" (74). For Butler (1993), gender and sexuality result from social norms and cultural regulation. In other words, they come from a societal order that has achieved a faux sanctity in the population's collective consciousness (Butler 1993, 21). In this order, one cannot—or at least, should not—cross the boundaries categorizing and defining genders and sexualities. Indeed, this is the essential argument made by those who oppose the recognition of transgender and queer identities. In this vein, the Joker's critique of society's moral and judicial order extends against society's strict gender normativity.

The Joker's critique of the sexual and gender categorizations enforced by society becomes especially apparent, albeit symbolically so, about midway through the film. During one scene in *The Dark Knight*, the Joker infiltrates Harvey Dent's hospital room disguised as a female nurse, complete with wig and traditional nurse uniform. On the one hand, his malevolently motivated cross-dressing once again evokes the gender-confused killers typical of slasher films. On the other hand, the Joker here notably foregoes his preferred weapon of choice, and so relinquishes his phallic power in donning the role of a quasi-maternal archetype as the nurse. This donning of a maternal role while abjuring his phallic power initiates a site of "abjection at work" that, via the psychoanalytic motifs, demonstrates the arbitrary, constructed, and traversable boundaries between gender categories (Creed 2015, 44).

Associating the traditionally "unclean" with the "abject," Julia Kristeva (1982) defines *abject*, in short, as "the jettisoned object," that which one "permanently thrust[s] aside in order to live" (1982, 2–3). At risk of oversimplification, the abject is whatever one foregoes in order to enter society, or in Lacanian terms, that which one forsakes to pass from the Real into the Symbolic—"to each superego its abject" (Kristeva 1982, 2). *The Dark Knight*'s hospital scene utilizes this concept of the abject by portraying the Joker as a malevolent midwife initiating Harvey Dent's second birth as the villain Two-Face. This is Dent's jettison from society, becoming, in the Joker's own words, "a freak" alongside Batman and himself.

Before elaborating on this relation between the Joker, Dent, and Kristeva's abject, a brief overview of Harvey Dent's role in *The Dark Knight* may be necessary. Throughout the film, Harvey Dent epitomizes conventional masculine virtue. Strong-jawed and blue-eyed, he embodies traditionally desired masculine traits, e.g., ambition, initiative, reason, and emotional control. The golden boy of Gotham City's district attorney's office, he is dubbed "Gotham's white knight," and seems visually suited to portray a modern Prince Charming. But following the accident that disfigures half his face, and his subsequent conversation with the Joker inside Gotham General Hospital, Harvey Dent transforms into a complete reversal of all these characteristics. He is no longer virtuous, instead exacting vengeance on anyone loosely connected to his fiancé's death. He is so given to a total sway of his vengeful passion that he foregoes reason by deciding the fate of every victim with the flip of a coin, chance as the only fair force in life. He ethically transforms from the manifestation of masculine virtue and a government-sanctioned enforcer of the moral order, for which Batman likewise fights, into the Joker's moral mimic.

This shift in character appropriately accompanies a shift in signification. No longer Harvey Dent, he has become Two-Face, named after his divided visage. As Barbara Creed (2015) writes, "the concept of a border is central to the construction of the monstrous in the horror film; that which crosses or threatens to cross the 'border' is abject" (42). To this end, Harvey's mutilated face visualizes this very border—one half is the Symbolic masculine, the other, primal flesh, the feminine Real. "The ultimate in abjection is the corpse," and Harvey's dual-natured physiognomy displays the borderland between the superego and the abject (Creed 2015, 40). One side is the celebrated masculinity of heteronormative, patriarchal culture—that embodied by Harvey Dent—the other, the very image of abjection itself, "which is the corpse, whole and mutilated" (Creed 2015, 42). Symbolically, Harvey Dent has shifted from his quintessential masculine state within society's Apollonian structure and descended into a monstrously feminized existence outside society.

Yet Dent has not totally entered the Joker's Dionysian realm. Unlike the Joker, Dent never advocates absolute amorality, but only the self-proclaimed righteousness of his vendetta. Kristeva (1982) writes, "he who denies morality is not abject; there can be grandeur in amorality and even in crime that flaunts its disrespect for the law" (4). By contrast, she defines the abject as

> the traitor, the liar, the criminal with a good conscience, the shameless rapist, the killer who claims he is a savior[. . . .] Any crime, because it draws attention to the fragility of the law, is abject, but premeditated crime, cunning murder, hypocritical revenge are even more so because they heighten the display of such fragility. (Kristeva 1982, 4)

This is Harvey's altered persona. Upon becoming Two-Face, Harvey Dent abandons reason's control and his judicial ambition to enlist in the malefic service of chance. He purports to enact a fair justice but, given his killings only target those connected to his fiancé's death, he evidences merely an obsession with vengeance. He becomes a traitor to Gotham's judicial system and to Batman as the supernatural executor of justice and order. Talking with Batman near the film's end, the Joker claims of Dent, "I lowered him down to our level." No doubt, through abjectification, this is precisely what the Joker does. Jettisoned from society, Dent becomes an outcast, joining the Joker and Batman as a "freak," cast from society like a leper as he operates in the shadows.

The Joker's self-purported purpose for corrupting Dent, as claimed in his final confrontation with Batman, is to reveal the artificiality of the judicial system's morality. If he can turn Harvey Dent, MVP of the district attorney's office, to evil then Gotham's citizens will lose all faith in the judicial process because the Joker will have revealed the moral code and its enforcers as a bad joke. His abjectification of Dent does the same to gender as well. By symbolically "feminizing" the quintessentially masculine Harvey Dent, Ledger's Joker "moves the conception of gender off the ground of a substantial model of identity to one that requires a conception of gender as a constituted *social temporality*" (Butler 1990, 140–41). If the Joker can sway Dent from masculine order into feminine chaos then that masculinity may never have been innate to Dent, but a mere social image. In other words, Dent's masculinity, and perhaps his heterosexuality, was never fixed. Through abjectifying Dent, the Joker's "versatile rationality and obscene sensuality [. . . become] taboo-breaking assaults on some hierarchical mythological order," specifically the notion of a stable and individuated identity perpetuated through Western society's categorizations of gender and sexuality (Zucker 1954, 311–12). Much like morality, the Joker confronts the arbitrary nature of society's sexual classifications.

This opposition to a stable identity by Ledger's Joker can be understood as inducing a historical trauma, as conceived by Kaja Silverman in *Male Subjectivity at the Margins* (1992). She speaks of historical trauma as the disruption of a given society's dominant fiction, which is "the ideological belief [through which] a society's 'reality' is constituted and sustained, and [through which] a subject lays claim to a normative identity" (Silverman 1992, 15). For Silverman (1992), dominant fictions foster "collective identifications and desires [. . .] which are first and foremost constitutive of sexual difference" (54). In this way, dominant fictions produce individuation by establishing categories of the normative and nonnormative and producing classifications used to differentiate sexual and gender differences. Historical traumas, by disrupting a society's dominant fiction disrupt that society's notions of gender and sexual differences. The trauma is not overtly sexual in nature. It may be an attack on the state and economic system, e.g., 9/11, but its traumatic residue reaches out into society's notions of gender and sexuality. Through this disruption, historical traumas reveal "the vulnerability of conventional masculinity and the larger dominant fiction," that of a patriarchal heteronormativity (Silverman 1992, 53).

The terrorist-Joker's corruption of Harvey Dent initiates a related historical trauma within the film, symbolically disrupting the dominant fiction of stable and compartmentalized sexual and gender identity embodied by characters like Harvey Dent and enforced by Batman. In the film's final minutes, following Harvey's short-lived spree of vengeance, Police Commissioner Jim Gordon stands beside Batman over Harvey's dead body and says, "The Joker won. Harvey's prosecution, everything he fought for—undone. Whatever chance you gave us of fixing our city dies with Harvey's reputation. We bet it all on him. The Joker took the best of us and tore him down. People will lose hope." In corrupting Harvey Dent, the Joker attacks Gotham's judicial system as well as Harvey's stable image as a steadfast and righteous public servant, and with both of these, Gotham's collective hope. As revealed in the film's psychoanalytical undertones, the Joker's attack on this ideological triptych extends not only to the vulnerability of conventional masculinity, but to stable notions of masculinity and sexuality altogether. The Joker's simultaneous moral corruption and abjectification of Harvey Dent exposes the frailty behind society's purportedly stable structures of morality, gender, and sexuality.

The Joker's Dionysian gospel opposes rules and categorizations in any form—"the only sensible way to live in this world is without rules," he says. If society's moral code is a bad joke, why not it's gender code as well? His Dionysian philosophy aims to "cross the boundaries of individuation [. . . and holds that] individuation is the primal source of all evil" (Nietzsche 2016, 50–51). Just as with the categories of good and evil, so categories of hetero/homo, cis/trans, and normative/nonnormative do not exist in nature. The

Joker's amoral crusade advocates the destruction of all categorization and rules, whether moral or sexual, believing them unnatural and irrational. He wants the return to a primordial, Dionysian chaos. As he tells Harvey Dent, "I'm a dog chasing cars. . . . I just do things." Ultimately, what he wants from the world is the abandonment of all order and classifications and a return to unbridled being in which people simply do without the compulsive need to categorize deeds or identity as good/evil, hetero/homo, queer/normative, and so on. He does not want the deconstruction of binaries, but the abolition of all individuating categorization.

Understanding the Joker's erotic violence as dramatized sadomasochism reinforces this abolition of sexual individuation. Sadomasochism has long been understood as a politically subversive practice since "masochism is always politically charged" (Muller 2014, 3). In fact, one of its political potentials being its "rupture in the link between identities and citizenships [that] stands in contrast to feminist and lesbian/gay/bisexual/transgender claims and the identity politics fueling such works" (Landridge 2006, 381). Many who participate in sadomasochistic practices "in no way identify themselves with sadomasochistic identities or communities" (Landridge 2006, 381). In this, sadomasochism "allows for an alternate formation of subjectivity by offering new possibilities (separate from modernity's sexual ethos of surveillance, discipline, and control) for being and relating to others" (Muller 2014, 10). The Joker offers no reason for audiences to identify him as exclusively male/female, hetero/homo, or queer/normative. Unlike these categories, sadomasochism does not constitute one's identity according to practitioners. Sadomasochism is not something one is, but rather something one does, and as the Joker says, "I just do things." In this, the Joker's eroticized violence reinforces his crusade against societal individuation, his rally cry for the termination of all categorization and order, for a world in which gender and sexuality, as well as morality cease to function as meaningful categories.

Such a sadomasochistic lens reinforces the Joker's ambiguous gender and mercurial sexuality. The donning of various gender roles in masochistic practices, according to Torkild Thanem and Louise Wallenberg (2010), makes for the transgression of gender differences "by becoming not man and not woman, but both." It is "a specific suspension of differences, somewhere between unity and a longed-for radical diversity and multiplicity" (Thanem and Wallenberg 2010). This donning of gender roles applies equally to the Joker. Twice in the film, the Joker dresses in something other than his normal attire, once as a female nurse in a wig and white dress uniform, and another time as a male police officer sans makeup. In all of these cases, much as the sadomasochistic practitioner, the Joker openly acts a violent part, whether as the Joker, a male police officer, or female nurse. In doing so, he shows himself capable of passing as all genders, and perhaps as none. The Joker's ambiguous gender, perpetuated both through his appearance and quasi-sadomasochistic practices, latently oppose the strict gender classifications enforced in normative notions of a stable sexual identity by preventing him from being classified exclusively as either man or woman, always retaining the potential for either.

About midway through *The Dark Knight*, the Joker is captured by Gotham City Police. Upon having the Joker searched per protocol, the mayor asks Commissioner Jim Gordon what they have learned about the Joker so far. Gordon answers, "Nothing. No matches on prints, DNA, dental. Clothing is custom, no labels. Nothing in his pockets but knives and lint. No name. No other alias." This summarizes the Joker. He cannot be classified as any specific person or thing because he abjures all individuating classifications; he only is. His nonsignification becomes his signification. He stands for unindividuated being, his mission being "the attempt to cross the fixed boundaries of individuation" (Nietzsche 2016, 50). His political and sexual allegiances are too mercurial to identify in any exclusive or definite terms so that he appears to possess none at all. He represents pure, uncategorized being, and his goal, as voiced by Alfred in echo of George W. Bush, is to remake the world after his image. In short, the Joker's mercurial gender and sexuality accompanied by his erotic violence confront and oppose the very notion of a fixed sexual or gender identity.

As mentioned during this essay's introduction, Ledger's Joker, and Christopher Nolan's film in which he appears, to this day retains unofficial status as a gold standard among fans. Following Alfred's summation of the character in the film, Ledger's Joker is spoken of as an amoral terrorist figure engaging in chaotic violence for its own sake. In challenging once-stable beliefs of morality and state, the Joker likewise confronts any idea of a stable gender or sexuality. It is my suspicion that this latent confrontation is a part of Ledger Joker's resonance with audiences. His every action, indeed his every existence, challenges dominant fictions proliferating in America. He demonstrates an alternative, yet demonized, way of being contrary to the cleanly categorized and individuated mode of Western society. He represents all of the freedom and difficulty, the laughter and horror, of living without classifications, categories, or any individuation whatsoever. Frank Miller may be right to call the Joker a homophobic nightmare (Sharrett 1991, 36), but the Joker is also a secretly desired freedom. At once terror and laughter, he is what so many fear and long for.

REFERENCES

Baum, Bruce. 2009. "The Dark Knight (Warner Bros. Pictures 2008)." *New Political Science* 31, no. 2: 267–69.

Bush Jr., George W. 20 September 2001. "Address to a Joint Session of Congress and the American People." The White House Archives, United States Capitol, Washington, D.C. Accessed June 4, 2019. https://georgewbush-whitehouse.archives.gov/news/releases/2001/09/20010920-8.

Butler, Judith. 1990. *Gender Trouble: Feminism and the Subversion of Identity*. New York: Routledge.

———. 1993. "Critically Queer." *GLQ: A Journal of Lesbian and Gay Studies* 1, no. 1: 17–32.

Clover, Carol J. 2015. "Her Body, Himself: Gender in the Slasher Film." In *The Dread of Difference: Gender and the Horror Film*, edited by B. K. Grant, 68–115. Austin: University of Texas Press.

Crawford, Elizabeth. 1998. *The Women's Suffrage Movement: A Reference Guide 1866–1928*. London: UCL Press.

Creed, Barbara. 2015. "Horror and the Monstrous-Feminine: An Imaginary Abjection." In *The Dread of Difference: Gender and the Horror Film*, edited by B. K. Grant, 37–67. Austin: University of Texas Press.

Daniels, Lee. 1999. *Batman: The Complete History*. New York: Chronicle Books.

Evans, David T. 1993. *Sexual Citizenship: The Material Construction of Sexualities*. New York, NY: Routledge.

Freud, Sigmund. 1971a. *The Standard Edition of the Complete Works of Sigmund Freud, Vol. XI*, edited by James Strachey. London: Hogarth Press.

———. 1971b. *The Standard Edition of the Complete Psychological Works of Sigmund Freud, Vol. XXI*, edited by James Strachey. London: Hogarth Press.

Foucault, Michel. 1978. *The History of Sexuality, Volume 1: An Introduction*. Translated by Robert Hurley. New York: Pantheon.

Garneau, Eric. 2015. "Lady HaHa: Performativity, Super-Sanity, and the Mutability of Identity." In *The Joker: A Serious Study of the Clown Prince of Crime*, edited by Robert M. Peaslee and Robert G. Weiner, 33–48. Jackson: University Press of Mississippi.

Halberstam, Judith. 2005. *In a Queer Time and Place: Transgender Bodies, Subcultural Lives*. New York: New York University Press.

Hamm, Sam, Warren Skaaren, Jon Peters, Peter Guber, Tim Burton, Jack Nicholson, Michael Keaton, et al. 1989. *Batman*. Burbank, Calif: Warner Bros.

Hassoun, Dan. 2015. "Shifting Makeups: The Joker as Performance Style from Romero to Ledger." In *The Joker: A Serious Study of the Clown Prince of Crime*, edited by R. M. Peaslee and R. G. Weiner, 3–18. Jackson: University Press of Mississippi.

Heit, Jamey. 2011. "No Laughing Matter: The Joker as a Nietzschean Critique of Morality." In *Vader, Voldemort, and Other Villains: Essays on Evil in Popular Media*, edited by Jamey Heit, 175–88. Jefferson: McFarland.

Kristeva, Julia. 1982. *Powers of Horror: An Essay in Abjection*. New York: Columbia University Press.

Landridge, Darren. 2006. "Voices from the Margins: Sadomasochism and Sexual Citizenship." *Citizenship Studies* 10, no. 4: 373–89.

Mencken, H. L. 2006. *The Philosophy of Friedrich Nietzsche*. New York: Barnes and Noble.

Muller, Christine. 2011. "Power, Choice, and September 11 in *The Dark Knight*." In *The 21st Century Superhero: Essays on Gender, Genre, and Globalization in Film*, edited by R. J. Gray II and B. Kaklamanidou, 46–59. Jefferson: McFarland.

Muller, Amber Jamilla. 2014. *Sensational Flesh: Race, Power, and Masochism*. New York: NYU Press.

Nichols, Michael. 2011. "'I Think You and I Are Destined to Do This Forever': A Reading of the Batman/Joker Comic and Film Tradition through the Combat Myth." *The Journal of Religion and Popular Culture* 23, no. 2: 236–50.

Nietzsche, Friedrich. 2016. *The Birth of Tragedy and Other Writings*. Edited by Raymond Geuss and Ronald Speirs. Translated by Ronald Speirs. Cambridge Texts in the History of Philosophy. Cambridge: Cambridge University Press.

Nolan, Christopher, Jonathan Nolan, David S. Goyer, Emma Thomas, Charles Roven, Morgan Freeman, Michael Caine, et al. 2012. *The Dark Knight Rises*. Burbank, CA: Warner Home Video.

Puar, Jasbir. 2005. "Queer Times, Queer Assemblages." *Social Text* 23, nos. 3–4: 121–39.

Richardson, Louise. 2007. *What Terrorists Want: Understanding the Enemy, Containing the Threat*. New York: Random House.

Rodriquez, Mario. 2014. "Physiognomy and Freakery: The Joker on Film." *Americana: The Journal of American Popular Culture (1900–present)* 13, no. 2: http://www.americanpopularculture.com/journal/articles/fall_2014/rodriguez.htm.

Sharrett, Christopher. 1991. "Batman and the Twilight of the Idols: An Interview with Frank Miller." In *The Many Lives of Batman: Critical Approaches to a Superhero and His Media*, edited by R. E. Pearson and W. Uricchio, 33–46. New York: Routledge.

Silverman, Kaja. 1992. *Male Subjectivity at the Margins*. New York: Routledge.

Thanem, Thorkild and Louis Wallenberg. 2010. "Buggering Freud and Deleuze: Toward a queer theory of masochism." *Journal of Aesthetics & Culture* 1, no. 1: https://www.tandfonline.com/doi/abs/10.3402/jac.v2i0.4642.

Wertham, Fredric. 1954. *Seduction of the Innocent: The Influence of Comic Books on Today's Youth*. New York: Rinehart & Company.

Williams, Linda. 1992. "Gender, Genre, and Excess." *Film Quarterly* 44, no. 4: 2–13.

Wood, Robin. 1978. "The Return of the Repressed." *Film Comment* 14, no. 4: 24–32.

Yuval-Davis, Nira. 2008. *Gender and Nation*. London: Sage.

Zucker, Wolfgang M. 1954. "The Image of the Clown." *The Journal of Aesthetics and Art Criticism* 12, no. 3: 310–17.

———. 1967. "The Clown as the Lord of Disorder." *Theology Today* 24, no. 3: 306–17.

Chapter Five

There are Different Ways of Being Strong

Steven Universe *and Developing a Caring Superhero Masculinity*

Julian Barr, David J. Roberts, and Edgar Sandoval

Is care a superpower? For men like Batman, Captain America, and Superman the answer might be no. In general, superheroes have an origin story—through family tragedy, biomedical accident, or circumstance of birth—followed by a specific development trajectory that shapes their purpose, powers, and universes. Within these dominant narratives, superheroes physically incapacitate their opponents in order to become victorious. Their muscular bodies mark them as bearers of masculine power over villains who frequently scheme or engage in more feminine forms of politics (Brown 1999; Roblou 2012; Avery-Natale 2013; Fawaz 2016). Throughout the superhero genre, including those tailored to children, superheroes must dominate their opponents to signal their strength. But what if their strength was measured by how much they care for others? What if we root for the villain to be improved instead of destroyed? In this chapter, we argue that care as power challenges hegemonic representations of masculinity within the superhero genre in productive ways.

Debuting in 2013, Cartoon Network's *Steven Universe* (*SU*) entered the realm of the superhero genre as a coming-of-age tale about a thirteen-year-old boy and his adventures with the Crystal Gems (CGs), a group of femme-identifying extraterrestrial rebels protecting Earth from the Diamonds, the leaders of their planet, known as Homeworld. The show airs alongside other superhero-driven programs on Cartoon Network, including *Teen Titans Go, OK KO, Ben 10*, and *Adventure Time*. These shows all, at least partially, focus on a male hero fighting and defeating villains. *SU* offers a different spin on the genre through a hero whose strength comes not from a dominating masculinity, but rather from compassion and support for friends—and even foes.

Within media studies, the examination of the relationship between masculinity and media first came to focus in the 1970s (Hanke 1998). Feminist, critical race, queer, and trans scholars have additionally explored masculinity as a dominant cultural identity and invisible norm. Raewyn Connell (1987; 1990) first introduced the concept of "hegemonic masculinity" as a form of masculinity that becomes common sense and idealized in modern society. While many masculinities exist alongside and challenge this dominating form, hegemonic masculinity exists precisely because other forms of masculinity are considered weaker or subordinate (Connell 1995). These "alternative" forms of masculinity (such as gay or Black, but not limited to them) have the capacity to leave unchallenged the central aspects of masculinity that reaffirm a gendered hierarchy in society (Myers 2012). Since children's television shows often represent these hierarchies, "everyday children will police each other in ways that they see on television" (Myers 2012, 141). Shows have long-lasting effects on what children learn and do in the world. *SU* offers a radically different representation of a caring masculinity that actively challenges domination as its premise.

While some contemporary depictions of superheroes have represented them as more whimsical or emotional than their predecessors, these characters do not diverge far from traditional narratives of masculinity before returning to similar tropes. Men continue to be the protagonists while women play a supportive role, upholding masculinist frameworks within superhero narratives (Kvaran 2017). While superheroes may experience traits considered feminine (such as hysteria, loss, etc.), they are often recuperated through the conquest of their opponents or obstacles. For example in *Batman: The Killing Joke*, Batman is driven to extreme violence after the Joker paralyzes Batgirl and tortures Commissioner Gordon. Drawing on our interpretations as viewers, we argue that a superhero masculinity that embraces care can depict an alternative comprehension of being strong that can rewrite many violent tropes. Superheroes communicating with empathy and who seek understanding can be made legible as valuable skills for developing men within a genre that valorizes violence and domination in its ensemble of male superheroes.

Caring masculinities do not have a singular form nor are they unproblematic (Elliott 2016; England and Dyck 2016). The juxtaposition of caring masculinities with superheroes raises a significant concern about how "protection" is understood, as seen in fictional constructions (Dittmer 2012) and the real world (Cuomo 2013). Within a narrative where the superhero must save people, they tend to focus on the physical aspect of the situation to ensure minimal injury and death of those deemed innocent. The superhero saves someone from danger, swiftly deals with villains, and protects their loved ones from those who seek their destruction. Nonviolence is rarely the solution to a problem. Protection becomes constructed discursively and materially within masculinist frameworks. Contrary to these depictions, this chapter emphasizes a relational form of caring that seeks to move beyond physical security toward one that examines power within our relationships to each other.

A feminist ethics of care informs our understanding of how caring masculinities use emotions to expand how we understand protection. Carol Gilligan (1982) and Nel Noddings (1982) are attributed to the rise of care ethics as a distinct moral theory that critiqued other approaches that held a masculine bias. Care ethics has been taken up, challenged, and further developed by other scholars. Such scholars often draw on a feminist ethic to further examine bias within moral theory (Baier 1989; Kittay and Meyers 1987; Ruddick 1989; Tronto 1993; Held 2006). A specific feminist ethics of care proposes an examination of the power-related implications in the association between gender and care, remains attentive to masculine and other biases, understands individual action within the context of social practices, and illuminates the differences in who engages in these kinds of caring practices (Jaggar 1991). Virginia Held (2006) suggests that "the ethics of care values emotion rather than rejects it[. . . . S]uch emotions as sympathy, empathy, sensitivity, and responsiveness are seen as the kind of moral emotions that need to be cultivated" (10). Held (2016) argues that the concept of care extends beyond close familial and friendly relations to "the bonds on which political and social institutions can be built, and even to the global concerns that citizens of the world can share" (30–31).

A feminist ethics of care provides insight into the possibilities that caring masculinities provide, possibilities that ought not be limited to physical security for bystanders. Karla Elliott (2016) proposes that "caring masculinities can be seen as masculine identities that exclude domination and embrace the affective, relational, emotional, and interdependent qualities of care identified by feminist theorists of care. There is no place for these positive emotions in dominating hegemonic masculinity" (252–53). Caring masculinities recast protection as a masculine value into "relational, interdependent, care-oriented ones" (Elliott 2016, 253). As we subsequently explore, Steven Universe, the protagonist, embodies this form of caring masculinity. He primarily supports the CGs through defensive and supportive powers: healing, shield proficiency, phytokinesis, empathetic telepathy, and others. Early on in the show, Steven attempts to befriend instead of defeat a monster. Through gestures of care (offering food or communicating), Steven chooses to develop a connection with his enemies. He does not want to dominate them through violence because he cares for and about them. In being open about his vulnerabilities and caring for others, Steven's journey to understand the connection between his power, care, and his relationship with others makes visible the importance of work outside of battles, and after disaster. It places value on questions of responsibility and community within the superhero's world and, ultimately, in ours.

Multiple representations of gender play a significant role within *SU* to allow for a caring masculinity to emerge. Rebecca Sugar created *SU* because she recognized that a majority of other children's animated shows do not take expansive approaches to presenting gender. Sugar, as gender nonbinary, seeks to move away from the dominant representation of the gender binary that is generally found in popular culture. This motivated her to develop a show that features many of the tropes of superheroes while simultaneously focusing on emotional growth, thereby challenging several gendered conventions within the genre. Gems do not have real, physical bodies; their bodies are illusions, projections of light. Gems construct these projections of light, whether through their individual decision or as told by the authority on Homeworld. Sugar explains that the Gems are gender expansive since their bodies are constructions. The intricacies of this gender play have been explored theoretically, pointing to gender as a form of performance instead of biological (Dunn 2016). In this way, Gems do not adhere to strict, rigid, and binary categorizations of gender but explore how variously gendered traits operate together. The show centers femininity in that it portrays Steven as caring and supportive alongside an entire species that are feminine-presenting.

Sugar represents gender expansively in *SU*, queering many human gender norms. We have interpreted these norms in the show in conjunction with interviews conducted with Sugar. Most humans in the show follow what we consider to be gender norms insofar as most are portrayed as cisgender and keep to gendered expectations. Some humans have struggled with this, such as when Sadie feels uncomfortable being forced to wear a dress by her mother ("Sadie's Song"). Gems, who are seemingly not confined to Earth's standards, further challenge gender norms. The Gems come from Homeworld, which hosts a matriarchal society ruled by the Diamonds. By Earth's standards, all Gems would be assumed to be female in their outward manifestations (clothing, voice style, and physical appearance), including representations ranging from butch (such as Jasper) to more traditional femininities (such as Aquamarine).

When Earth gender norms do influence the Gems, they perform gender differently by adopting the norms to meet their needs. For example, when Ruby and Sapphire got married, Ruby wore a traditional wedding dress while Sapphire had on a tuxedo. Generally, Ruby dons pants while Sapphire wears a dress, demonstrating that the Gems continue to challenge Earth norms while appreciating what some human practices have to offer. In this way, Gems challenge norms associated with men and women, aligning with scholarly understandings of gender as fluid and performative (Butler 1990; Browne and Nash 2016; Dunn 2016). *SU* approaches superhero masculinity through an expansive depiction of gender, troubling the binaries between men and women. For instance, we believe the representation of the matriarchal society of Gems engaging in colonial and imperial practices challenges the image that women are inherently less violent, demonstrating that some of Steven's biggest conflicts stem from the Diamond's own destructive power. These various representations of gender enable a caring form of masculinity to emerge for Steven.

THE MAGICAL WORLD OF *STEVEN UNIVERSE*

As self-appointed defenders and protectors of Earth from the ravages of the Diamond's colonial and imperial legacies, the Gems hold the fate of the world in their hands. The show follows the Gems, a team consisting of Steven, Pearl, Garnet, and Amethyst. Thousands of years prior, under the leadership of Steven's extraterrestrial mother, Rose Quartz, the original Gems led a rebellion against Homeworld. This planet was dominated by a colonial authority known as the Diamonds, whose primary objective was extracting resources from other planets. Rose eventually sacrificed herself to create Steven with her human partner Greg Universe. *SU* tracks Steven's development under the care of the CGs and Greg in Beach City, where they live. During the course of the show, Steven grows into his role as a supportive protector of his friends, family, Beach City, and Earth.

Steven's narrative follows a similar trajectory to those of other superheroes. His origin story becomes his passion as he embraces his heroic role. Steven is half-human and half-Gem, and the first male Gem according to Sugar's (2014) comments in a Reddit Ask-Me-Anything. While Steven starts off as a kind, lighthearted adolescent, he takes his role in the CGs seriously when he learns that his mother shattered (the Gem equivalent of killing) one of the Diamonds. He believes he must take responsibility for the consequences of his mother's actions and, thus, sacrifices himself to protect those around him, even though those same individuals want to stand with him against the threat of Homeworld ("Dewey Wins"). Steven comes to understand that Rose staged a rebellion against Homeworld to protect life on Earth and wants to fight with his friends against the Diamonds. While Steven initially took on a solitary approach other superheroes adopt, subsequent episodes track how Steven learns that his friends and the CGs want to support him as a team, and he eventually realizes that is a better approach.

The inhabitants of Beach City additionally shape Steven's development as a superhero. He becomes close friends with another adolescent, Connie, a woman of color who enjoys reading and studying. Connie serves as one of Steven's primary connections to the human world though he is friends with other humans, and the show consistently demonstrates how he improves his friendships with them. The show also illustrates how the CGs and Beach City townspeople interact with each other, exploring the joys and difficulties of a town frequently under threat by extraterrestrial forces. Steven is not detached or separate from all the inhabitants of Beach City. After disasters, he does more than help physically remove the remnants of invasion; he cares for the residents who experience distress or trauma. They support Steven in intimately understanding human emotion, which in turn helps him develop his powers.

The importance of Steven caring about and for his family and friends is underscored by the possibility of "Gem Fusion" within *SU*. The process of "Gem Fusion," a magical construction in which Gems fuse their bodily projections together, demonstrates the centrality of embracing "positive emotion, interdependence, and relationality" (Elliott 2016, 256). This enables the possibility for a caring superhero masculinity counter to the more traditional hegemonic depictions of superheroes. We argue that Fusions serve to challenge the idea of a muscular, autonomous superhero body in favor of a body more malleable and attentive to emotions. Fusion offers insights into broader conversations about consent, communication, and healthy/unhealthy relationship dynamics between friends and lovers. Steven's ability to fuse with Connie, a human, to become Stevonnie allows him to perceive his identity as a relationship with another. As explained earlier, the Gems do not possess inherent gendered identities because their bodies are light projections from their physical gemstones. *SU* asserts that Gems' bodies are "human constructs" ("Reformed") and "only an illusion" ("Fusion Cuisine"). When their bodies are damaged, they retreat to their physical gems where they reconstruct their bodies, altering their bodies if desired. When *SU* introduces fusion, Pearl and Amethyst engage in a semierotic dance to fuse their light projections together. Ruby describes this process as "intimate," and *SU* consistently engages with the themes of trust and consent as integral to fusion ("Keystone Motel").

The Fusions, the combination of fused Gems, are a new formation, rather than being one Gem or the other ("Log Date 7 15 2"). Eli Dunn (2016) describes Fusions as the epitome of agender and genderqueer representation whereby the process of fusion is a type of performance that "undermines the dominant order of the corporeal body, equating the physical substance of the body not with a fixed, rigid or imposing structure but as something malleable, combinable and more powerful in its enactment of fluidity" (49). While most Gems can and do change their bodies at will, it is through fusion that the individual body is destroyed in favor of combining with another being. Rather than hold individual autonomy as foundational to the strength of a superhero, the ultimate strength in *SU* relies on healthy relationships between characters. The process of fusion depends on trust between the Gems to remain stable ("Jail Break"), confronting their conflicts with honest emotional communication ("Mindful Education").

Within the world of *SU*, fusion had not previously occurred between two different types of Gems until Garnet, the Fusion made from Ruby and Sapphire ("The Answer," "Now We're Only Falling Apart"). Within Homeworld's norms, Garnet challenged the constitutive material and discursive processes where Gem Fusion existed strictly between the same kind of Gems (i.e., a Ruby with another Ruby). The Diamond Authority only used fusion between two of the same Gems to increase the strength of their colonization efforts elsewhere. Garnet represents a Fusion for the purpose of love instead of violence, which is against what the Diamonds believe the purpose of fusion should be. Garnet challenges the norms of Homeworld to continue living as herself on Earth, as many queer and trans people must do when their families do not accept them. Similarly, she must leave behind her home to live as the Fusion she is. The Fusion between two different Gems, or humans, means that emotions play a significant role in the process. If fusion serves as a site of bodily malleability, the process similarly subverts the distinction between body and mind. The Fusion cannot exist if the Gems are not of the same state of mind. The characters of *SU* must work through their emotions or differences as a prerequisite to maintain a stable Fusion. For example, Ruby initially only fused with other Rubies because the Diamonds forced their soldiers to do so. Ruby's decision to fuse with Sapphire testifies to the importance of choice within this new purpose for fusion.

While Garnet is her own entity, Ruby and Sapphire have had struggles in their relationship. They broke up after discovering that Rose Quartz had been lying about her true identity to the CGs, casting doubt on Rose's affirmations of their relationship being the answer to create different ways of being ("The Answer"). After some personal self-reflection and conversations with Steven, Ruby asks Sapphire to marry her because, as she states, "This way we can be together, even when we're apart! This time, being Garnet will be our decision" ("The Question"). While critiques have labeled marriage as a heteropatriarchal institution, Gems do not have weddings on Homeworld. For Gems, their temporal frame for history differs from that of humans. It is within this understanding that Garnet states, in reference to the wedding, "Humans found a way to make a moment's decision last forever" ("Reunited").

Conversely, a Fusion formed under negative emotions enables an analysis of harm within fusion. Fusion is both a site of violence and love. The first time the audience comes across fusion as a site of violence is after Pearl tricked Garnet into fusing with her. In "A Cry for Help," the CGs believe that an enemy was repairing a previously destroyed Communication Hub to communicate with Homeworld. Despite their efforts, they cannot track down the enemy. Steven and Amethyst, however, learn that another member of the CGs, Pearl, had been fixing the tower herself because she wanted to keep feeling the strength she experiences when she fuses with Garnet. Pearl had lied to Garnet, who feels that her trust was betrayed since fusion is an intimate process for her. The show carefully accounts for how Pearl had to respect the space that Garnet required and how she worked to earn back Garnet's trust.

Malachite is another example of an unstable Fusion. When Peridot—one of Homeworld's scouts—returns to Beach City with her guard Jasper and prisoner Lapis Lazuli, they attempt to capture the rebel CGs to hold them accountable for Rose Quartz shattering Pink Diamond. After the CGs escape their spaceship, Jasper encourages Lapis to fuse with her to defeat them, telling her that fusion "is your chance to take revenge" ("Jail Break"). Lapis agrees but takes control over the Fusion Malachite, using water chains to drag the Fusion into the ocean as she yells, "Now you're my prisoner, and I'm never letting you go!" Surprised, Garnet states, "Yikes. They are really bad for each other." She claims that the Fusion is unstable and could break at any moment. After Malachite splits up, Lapis and Steven become friends. In "Alone at Sea," Steven takes Lapis on a boat to rekindle her love for water. Lapis shares that she cannot stop thinking about battling with Jasper as Malachite. Jasper suddenly climbs onto the deck of the boat, asking Lapis to fuse with her again. Lapis hesitates, stating that she hates how much she enjoyed taking her anger out on Jasper. The Fusion Malachite demonstrates the realities of a toxic relationship. However, Steven does not treat Lapis like a fragile victim in need of protecting. Instead, Steven respectfully seeks to understand Lapis and provides space for her to be honest about her feelings regarding Jasper. The mainstay of fusion means that Steven must be attentive to the social relations between other characters if he wants to create strong, resilient, and caring communities.

Steven has also experienced the joys and struggles of fusion through the Fusion Stevonnie. Eli Dunn (2016) notes that Stevonnie is deliberately genderqueer and does not feel "strange or out of place in their physical body" (53). Stevonnie's experience in Beach City, through their subversive gendered play (as genderqueer), opens up different, and sometimes negative, social experiences based upon that gender play. For example, Stevonnie meets a self-proclaimed "cool" teenage boy named Kevin at a rave they agreed to attend together. Kevin asks them to dance, expecting a yes, and continues to ask even though Stevonnie has made it clear that they did not want to dance with him. Dunn argues that, "Stevonnie's interaction with Kevin at the dance is one in which they are sexualized, even despite their protests. Kevin sees Stevonnie as a sexual object, he even tries to pull them back on to the dance floor" (54). They become uncomfortable with his insistence and reluctantly agree, ultimately unfusing after a few moments of throwing their fists around and stomping there feet. Steven and Connie appear relieved to be apart, laughing and dancing together. Stevonnie enables Steven to learn about the mixed experiences, both positive and negative, that Dunn (2016) argues genderqueer people experience in their everyday lives.

While Steven connects with others without needing to fuse with them, his Fusion with Connie as Stevonnie serves to develop a formation of the self that relies on relationality and interdependence. Steven rarely fights himself but fuses with Connie to rely on her sword skills to defend himself, them, their friends, and the inhabitants of Earth.

STEVEN'S HEROIC PURPOSE

Steven, in many ways, does not follow the traditional model of the masculine superhero (Fusion is a prime example of this), yet he follows common tropes of the superhero genre in unique ways, such as figuring out his role as a hero. The superhero genre is marked by similar heroic experiences around crime on the part of the protagonist, including stopping street crime as well as the grand schemes of supervillains. In *SU*, Steven similarly supports the inhabitants of Beach City. Instead of preventing crime, however, he helps them with everyday problems, such as when Pizza Place and Fry Restaurant had a turf war about food ("Restaurant Wars"). It is through these mundane conflicts that Steven develops his relationship with community members. No doubt, this inclusion signals that Steven attends to both the effects of spectacular events and the emotional struggles of everyday life. Through the major story arcs and the everyday issues he helps to resolve, Steven formulates an understanding of a hero that is supportive of his friends' lives and protects them from the destruction of Homeworld.

Steven, like many heroes in the superhero genre, struggles with who he is and where he comes from. His father, the CGs, and other Gems do not understand how Rose Quartz gave up her form to create Steven, sometimes believing that Rose has changed her form to resemble Steven. Rose's history with Homeworld, and the secrets she kept from those around her, have a significant impact on Steven's upbringing. Greg initially raised Steven but when his son began to demonstrate Gem abilities, he understandably allowed the CGs to take his place as primary caretakers and major decision-makers in Steven's life. Greg increasingly became involved as Steven grew and began to be immersed in the politics of the Gems and Homeworld. Although Steven struggles to understand himself as half-human and half-Gem, Greg provides advice and support as Steven forges his own path.

At the same time, Steven feels the pressure to develop his Gem powers and to initially take on a leadership role with the CGs because his mother was the previous leader. Steven's endeavors to be like his mother change when he learns that Rose had no expectations for him ("Lion 4: Alternate Ending"). Steven shifts from feeling that he had an obligation to be the leader of the CGs to share that responsibility with his team members. For example, after Steven explains why he wants the previously exiled Bismuth to join the Gems, Bismuth remarks that he has "Spoken like a leader." Steven caringly responds, "No. Spoken like a friend" ("Made of Honor"). Through the affirmation of his mother and others, Steven found that his purpose as a CG was not to lead them, like Rose did, but to support them.

While other superheroes approach conflict and their relationships in ways emblematic of hegemonic masculinity, Steven embraces a more caring understanding of his purpose as a hero. This displaces how society highly valorizes hegemonic patriarchal values and instead offers an entry point for men to consider other traits traditionally framed as feminine as valuable in their own right. He makes room for the positive emotions that hegemonic masculinity often excludes (Elliott 2016). This form of masculinity enables men to demonstrate their feelings and vulnerability, which resonates for many who do not see themselves in the body and actions of traditional superheroes.

As such, Steven's role as a caregiver and confidant to the Gems is a unique one. The Gems are characteristically strong, tactical warriors, each with a signature style: Garnet possesses super strength and uses gauntlets; Pearl uses her spear with speed and ease; and Amethyst specializes in utilizing her body and whip. They are rather aggressive when encountering problems when Steven first joins their adventures. Steven's approach to conflict differed despite being raised by the Gems and is, in part, tied to his supportive abilities. Throughout the show, Steven's role within the CGs develops as a caring counterbalance to the initial aggressive approach the team uses in their missions, focusing more on defense, advocating against violence, communicating, and healing. Regardless of how Steven understood his role within the CGs, he consistently aimed to de-escalate conflict before being forced to respond with violence (if at all). Steven's use of heroism seeks to account not only for the physical conditions of someone's life but also their emotional well-being, which reflects feminist scholars' suggestions to reimagine security in a broader sense. To this end, Dana Cuomo (2013) demonstrates how policing interventions into intimate partner violence are situated within narrow conceptions of masculinist protection that often both fail to meet the multiple needs of victims and disavow their autonomy.

One particularly good example of this broader sense of security is apparent in his willingness to listen to his opponents and taking time to determine if a violent response is necessary, whereas the CGs would destroy the bodily projection and place the gem in a prison-like state by bubbling them. This happens when Bismuth shares a Gem-shattering weapon that would kill the Diamonds with Steven. Steven refuses, stating, "It's not what a Crystal Gem would do" ("Bismuth"). His refusal triggers Bismuth's anger, and he desperately attempts to explain himself. As Bismuth becomes increasingly aggressive, attacking Steven, his approach does not immediately change despite being in physical danger. It is not until Bismuth tries to shatter Steven's Gem that he resorts to violence. He jabs his sword through Bismuth, bubbling her. While Steven resorted to violence for self-preservation, this decision leaves him emotionally devastated ("Mindful Education").

Steven's de-escalation approach has proved fruitful, as exemplified in his encounters with Centipeedle (also see "Ocean Gem," "Gem Drill," and "Reunited"). Centipeedle, later identified as Nephrite, worked as a commander during the Gem War on Earth before becoming corrupted when the Diamonds attacked. The process of corruption transforms Gems into monsters who respond to other beings with aggression. Nephrite appeared in the first episode as Centipeedle, and the Gems fight her, with Steven ultimately defeating her. However, in "Monster Buddies," Steven interacts with Nephrite again, approaching her with care and offering her food. After bonding through the day, Nephrite later injures herself protecting Steven from danger. Steven vows to discover how to use his healing powers to remove her corruption, which he attempts to do in "Monster Reunion." While he discovers that his powers alone are not strong enough to heal her corruption, this example illustrates Steven's commitment and compassion for others, even foes. Communication is foundational for de-escalation. Many real-world scenarios for everyday people can be dealt with in this way such as dealing with aggressive customers, drivers with road rage, and frustrated friends. Steven's approach arguably is unique within the superhero genre and the show itself.

Moreover, Steven's superpowers inform his role and purpose in the CGs. Discovered in "An Indirect Kiss," Steven has the ability to heal through his saliva. Within the superhero genre, healing is frequently associated as an ability only to heal themselves (for example, Wolverine and Deadpool)—though not exclusively as we do see male heroes in the X-Men world who have the ability to heal others. However, the genre does not often illustrate how heroes, their companions, and the city and its inhabitants actually recover from damage (Boampong 2016). Steven uses his ability to heal other Gems and humans, such as Pearl, Greg, and Connie. As revealed in "Off Colors," Steven's healing goes as far as resurrecting Lars when he is mortally injured on Homeworld. His ability to resurrect Lars, who subsequently turned pink, resonates with his Lion, who is also pink and possesses similar Gem abilities as Lars. Steven continues to care for his friends despite their distance, species, or orientation toward Homeworld.

Steven possesses other supportive powers that he uses in and outside of battle. Steven's empathetic telepathy enables him to fall asleep and enter a mindscape where he can interact with others, whether they are awake or in their dreams. When the Diamonds attack Earth in "Reunited," for example, Steven attempts to talk to them but is unable to reach them past their anger. After using his shield to protect the Gems from the Diamonds' blast, one of the Diamonds knocks him out. Steven enters a mental dreamscape where he provides supportive cheers to his fellow Gems and projects his emotional aura toward the Diamonds to confirm to them that he does, in fact, have Pink Diamond's Gem. In doing so, Steven appeals to the Diamonds through affective registers to protect Earth from their destructive anger.

Steven's powers define him as a superhero that centers protection, healing, and support in and outside of battle. This approach allows him to formulate his unique purpose within the Gems. Steven's superpowers offer a counterbalance to the more aggressive and battle-ready approach of the other Gems. While Steven's powers are, in many ways, extensions of his mother's, he forged a unique path toward developing himself as a member of the Gems. As opposed to using aggression or violence, he embodies a caring, relational, and affective approach to superhero masculinity, counter to the typical illustration of superhero masculinity that is aggressive and focused on defeating villains. Steven has made care his superpower and his main objective in conflict.

However, Steven takes his caring approach one step further. In between the episodes that tell the major arcs of the story, Steven and the Gems engage in everyday forms of heroics in Beach City. Steven cares for his friends' non-Gem-related conflicts and supports them materially. Steven learns from the inhabitants in Beach City, and he brings this lens to the Gems. Mainstream superheroes do intervene in day-to-day events, but the emotional support that occurs between major arcs is undeniably core to the show in a way that is unique. Even though television as a medium allows for these types of everyday moments to be depicted (more time), shows such as *Batman: The Animated Series* or *Avengers Assemble* do not take the time to illustrate the emotional care that occurs between characters, despite the episodes being twice as long as those in *SU*. While heroes often do not reflect or debrief over the resolved conflict, Steven does extend his care and time continuously outside of battle.

Steven's emotional support has become a central aspect of his role with the CGs. Almost every Gem character has had to deal with various issues including self-doubt, trauma, pain, and loss. Through it all, Steven is present to help them through these issues. He also indirectly brings more Gem refugees (Peridot and Lapis) to join the Gems through his caring approach, similar to that of his mother. Ultimately, Steven's goal is to be a friend to the Gems and not just a leader. For example, this manifests in his relationship with Pearl. Pearl, one of the original Gems and the first to rebel with Rose, was one of the strictest of the Gems with Steven as he grew up. Pearl fell in love with Rose and was by her side for thousands of years, ultimately suffering through the pain of lost love when Rose gives up her physical form to give birth to Steven. Rose, however, found love in Greg, Steven's father. Pearl initially perceived the relationship as a fling but eventually realized it was more. Consequently, Pearl began to resent Greg ("We Need to Talk"). When Rose and Greg decided to have Steven, Pearl lost Rose forever. She mostly avoided her grief, allowing it to transform into resentment toward Greg. Steven became aware of this and wanted to bring his family together. In "Mr. Greg," Steven insists that Pearl join him and Greg on a vacation to the big city. Greg and Pearl both appear anxious over this but agree for the sake of Steven. Through song, they both express their love for Rose and realize that their shared loss could have brought them closer together for mutual support.

Steven similarly supports the residents of Beach City. While Steven helps many townsfolk with various issues, his long-term support for the relationship between his friends Sadie and Lars continues to develop in complexity. They initially worked together at the Big Donut, where Steven noticed that Sadie had a crush on Lars. Steven believes they want to be together and later realizes that they each have issues to work out separately. First, Lars overcompensates when trying to appear cool in front of the other teenagers but eventually reveals that he is very insecure about himself. It should be noted that the trans and nonbinary fan base of the show have theorized that Lars is a trans man who was able to transition as a child but is still learning how to negotiate his masculinity (*I'm Just Saying* 2016). While the show's creators have not confirmed this theory, it demonstrates how Lars's emotional growth has connected with particular fans of the show whose own embodied experiences resonate with the on-screen depictions.

Secondly, Sadie often lacks self-confidence, partially due to her overbearing mother, but has shown her strength when facing enemies. While Steven originally seeks to get them together, he leaves that goal behind to focus on helping them both gain confidence in themselves. After Lars was kidnapped and became an outlaw space pirate, Steven reassures Sadie not to dwell on what she cannot control and encourages her to embrace her musical talents in Beach City ("Sadie Killer"). Additionally, Steven assists Lars in learning that he is brave and also helps him find a group of beings that accept him ("Lars' Head"). Not only does this story arc allow viewers to see the labor Steven puts in to support both of them, we also witness how Steven reflects on his actions and growth in his relationship to Sadie and Lars as a consequence. He shifted from seeing them as a potential couple that were just not connecting to understanding them as two individual people who needed support for themselves first.

STEVEN'S CARING MASCULINITY

Within the world of *SU*, care becomes a power that allows Steven to connect with the Gems and the foes that they face throughout the series. The Gems initially do not approach their foes with the same empathy that Steven possesses. The original members of the Gems' (Pearl and Garnet) approach to conflict is different because they fought against the colonizing efforts of Homeworld and viewed firsthand the Diamonds's potential for destruction. Steven's narrative arc parallels that of the coming-of-age adolescent with a focus on him becoming more empathetic and supportive as a character. In general terms, caring masculinities reject domination and its associated traits while embracing "values of care such as positive emotion, interdependence, and relationality" (Elliott 2016, 256). While Steven often draws on liberal concepts of autonomy, equality, and justice, Steven learns from the conflicts that arise when he does not account for others. He learns by noticing their frustration and talking with them about why they are hurt instead of just looking to fight the next villain.

His role throughout the show is a supportive one, but it is his ability to connect with others' emotions that shines through as his superpower. At the conclusion of *SU*'s television event "Diamond Days," the viewers realize that the Diamond's imperial efforts to extract resources and colonize other planets stemmed from their inability to see the world outside of their own perspective. Similar to how Western nations rationalize war, the genocide of Indigenous peoples, and the effects of climate change through a Western perspective, they often devalue and delegitimize other ways of knowing and being that do not align with their own. In the season finale, White Diamond decides to pull Steven's gem out of his body because she believes Pink Diamond has been hiding inside him. She refuses to recognize that Steven wants to be friends with "imperfect" Gems and inferior life beings, like humans. The separation of the gem from his body produces a Gem Steven and a human Steven, and White Diamond continues to refuse to accept that Steven and his Gem are in fact Steven. After human and Gem Steven are reunited together, White Diamond throws a tantrum and tells Steven that he is acting like a child, with Steven responding, "I am a child. What's your excuse" ("Change Your Mind")? He recommends to the embarrassed White Diamond that she might need to leave her own head if she wants to become familiar with the world outside and make things better. As a first step, Steven encourages the Diamonds to think about how their actions have impacted the lives of the corrupted Gems on Earth. Steven attempts to demonstrate that justifying one's use of violence against others also affects the people who have to carry out that violence.

SU's seeming commitment to providing viewers with a superhero whose characteristics, strengths, and powers embody those of caring masculinities challenges the strict rubric of hegemonic masculinity for superheroes. It provides a masculinity that is constituted by positive emotions, encouraging the perception of relationality and vulnerability with others as strengths instead of weaknesses. It places care at the center of a masculinity that arises through the representation of Steven. We do not claim that caring masculinities are new in superhero narratives. What we find particularly salient, however, is that Rebecca Sugar created *SU* to offer more expansive representations of gender within a television show. As nonbinary, Rebecca Sugar imbues meanings of masculinity that do not reinforce domination and its associated traits, but instead draws on those often associated with women and feminized emotions. She has brought in her identity as nonbinary to the superhero genre to show audiences a different type of superhero that can protect Earth while attending to the emotions of those around them, including those that mean to destroy the planet. This approach has connected the show with a diverse set of young, queer, trans, and nonbinary people who have become enthralled with *SU* for how the show emphasizes emotional growth and the power of care. The attractiveness of the show for LGBTQ peoples is that the CGs become a community where anyone, without disavowing their differences, can join. Ultimately, Steven's care becomes the conduit through which he is able to build relationships with others to defend Earth from Homeworld's destruction.

REFERENCE

Avery-Natale, Edward. 2013. "An Analysis of Embodiment among Six Superheroes in DC Comics." *Social Thought and Research* 32: 71–106.
Baier, Annette C.. 1989. "Hume, the Women's Moral Theorist?" *In Women and Moral Theory*, edited by Eva Feder Kittay and Diana T. Meyers. Totowa, NJ: Rowman & Littlefield.
Boampong, Jean. 2016. "Damage Control: Where Comic Books Meet Disaster Economics." *Bitch Media: Money Issue*, 2016.
Brown, Jeffrey A. 1999. "Comic Book Masculinity and the New Black Superhero." *African American Review* 33 (1): 25–42.
Browne, Kath, and Catherine Nash. 2016. *Queer Methods and Methodologies: Intersecting Queer Theories and Social Science Research*. New York: Routledge.
Butler, Judith. 1990. *Gender Trouble: Feminism and the Subversion of Identity*. New York: Routledge.
Connell, Raewyn. 1987. *Gender and Power: Society, the Person, and Sexual Politics*. Palo Alto, CA: Stanford University Press.
———. 1990. "An Iron Man: The Body and Some Contradictions of Hegemonic Masculinity." In *Sport, Men, and the Gender Order: Critical Feminist Perspectives*, edited by M. Messner and D. Sabo, 83–95. Champaign, IL: Human Kinetics Books.
———. 1995. *Masculinities*. Berkeley: University of California Press.
Cuomo, Dana. 2013. "Security and Fear: The Geopolitics of Intimate Partner Violence Policing." *Geopolitics* 18 (4): 856–74.
Dittmer, Jason. 2012. *Captain America and the Nationalist Superhero: Metaphors, Narratives, and Geopolitics*. Philadelphia: Temple University Press.
Dunn, Eli. 2016. "Steven Universe, Fusion Magic, and the Queer Cartoon Carnivalesque." *Gender Forum* 56: 44–57.

Elliott, Karla. 2016. "Caring Masculinities: Theorizing an Emerging Concept." *Men and Masculinities* 19 (3): 240–59.

England, Kim, and Isabel Dyck. 2016. "Masculinities, Embodiment and Care." In *Masculinities and Place*, edited by Andrew Gorman-Murray and Peter Hopkins, 285–97. New York: Routledge.

Fawaz, Ramzi. 2016. *The New Mutants: Superheroes and the Radical Imagination of American Comics*. New York: New York University Press.

Gilligan, Carol. 1982. *In a Different Voice*. Cambridge: Harvard University Press.

Hanke, Robert. 1998. "Theorizing Masculinity with/in the Media." *Communication Theory* 8 (2): 183–203.

Held, Virginia. 2006. *The Ethics of Care: Personal, Political, and Global*. New York: Oxford University Press.

I'm Just Saying. 2016. Trans Lars: The Masterpost. Tumblr. https://mostlyanything19.tumblr.com/post/147817674893/trans-lars-the-masterpost.

Jaggar, Alison M. 1991. "Feminist Ethics: Projects, Problems, Prospects." In *Feminist Ethics*, edited by C. Card, 78–104. Lawrence: University of Kansas Press.

Kittay, Eva Feder, and Diana T. Meyers, eds. 1987. *Women and Moral Theory*. Totowa, NJ: Rowman & Littlefield.

Kvaran, Kara M. 2017. "Super Daddy Issues: Parental Figures, Masculinity, and Superhero Films." *The Journal of Popular Culture* 50 (2): 218–38.

Myers, Kristen. 2012. "'Cowboy Up!': Non-Hegemonic Representations of Masculinity in Children's Television Programming." *Journal of Men's Studies* 20 (2): 125–43.

Noddings, Nel. 1982. *Caring: A Feminine Approach to Ethics and Moral Education*. Berkeley: University of California Press.

Roblou, Yann. 2012. "Complex Masculinities: The Superhero in Modern American Movies." *Culture, Society & Masculinities* 4 (1): 76–91.

Ruddick, Sara. 1989. *Maternal Thinking: Toward a Politics of Peace*. New York: Ballentine Books.

Sugar, Rebecca. 2014. "I Am Rebecca Sugar, Creator of Steven Universe, and Former Adventure Time Storyboarder, AMA!" Reddit Ask-Me-Anything. https://www.reddit.com/r/IAmA/comments/2e4gmx/i_am_rebecca_sugar_creator_of_steven_universe_and/.

Tronto, Joan C. 1993. *Moral Boundaries: A Political Argument for an Ethic of Care*. New York: Routledge.

Chapter Six

There Must Always Be a Thor

Marvel's Thor the Goddess of Thunder
and the Disruption of Heroic Masculinities

Kiera M. Gaswint

Jack Halberstam's (2004) examination of masculinity poses that maleness and masculinity are not synonymous. Instead, Halberstam (2004) argues that

> the masculinity of the white male relies on vast networks of secret government groups, well-funded scientists, the army, and an endless supply of both beautiful bad babes and beautiful good babes. Masculinity is primarily prosthetic and has little if anything to do with biological maleness and signifies more often as a technical special effect. (937)

This understanding of masculinity as a construct seems overly apparent while reading Halberstam's (2004) analysis. However, it is hard to think about this theory when Darcey in Marvel's *Thor* (2011) stares at Chris Hemsworth while he is changing clothes. "You know, for a homeless guy, he's pretty cut," she swoons, absorbing his body with her eyes. For men and women viewers alike, Darcey is pretty relatable in this moment. The cut, overly muscular male body is an all too common trope associated with male comic book characters since their earliest years. After all, is Superman even capable of being super without his fictitious rippling muscles? Darcey is simply sizing Thor up like the rest of us are—with muscles like that, it is hard to pick apart where Hemsworth's body begins and where his apparently oozing masculinity ends.

It seems like a no brainer that Thor is Norse mythology's image of hypermasculinity because of his body. Judith Butler (1987) understands that the body is important to the cultural portrayal of gender. Butler (1987) argues that "the body becomes a peculiar nexus of culture and choice, and [in] 'existing' one's body becomes a personal way of taking up and reinterpreting received gender norms" (38). Butler's (1987) point stresses the importance of the body as a reflection of gender norms, an all too common connection made in discussions about masculinity. "Indeed, when one looks at texts on masculinity and masculinity studies, the object of study is almost always male. This state of affairs disrupts the view of masculinity as a socially constructed phenomenon—it undercuts, more than 'somewhat,' the assertion that gender is not connected to sex" (Winnberg, Fahraeus, and Jonsson 2008, 1). It is easy to see where the separation between masculinity and biological maleness gets lost in a world that cinematically stresses the importance of the male body in relation to masculinity.

However, Halberstam's (2004) understanding of masculinity deeply contrasts this mode of thinking about gender. Halberstam (2004) demonstrates that the construction of heroic masculinity relies heavily on other peripheral objects, breaking the direct connection between biological sex and gender. This approach invites us to relocate the nexus of masculinity away from the body to the objects or people that create and reaffirm a character's masculinity. For example, Thor's weapon of choice Mjolnir, the hammer, is as famous as he is. Following Halberstam's (2004) assessment of masculinity then reveals that it is no surprise that Norse mythology's beacon of masculinity has always been coupled with a weapon that is particularly and embarrassingly phallic. In case Thor's body did not prescribe him as a man enough, Mjolnir certainly reaffirms Thor's masculinity not only by its shape, but also with an implied aptness for violence and war.

It is particularly interesting then that Marvel comics did something drastically different with their Thor comic book character in 2014 by relocating the nexus of masculinity from Thor Odinson altogether. Following the events of "Original Sin #8," Thor is unable to lift Mjolnir. In a turn of events that was largely unprecedented in Thor mythology, in "Thor: The Goddess of Thunder #1," Jane Foster lifts Mjolnir from the ground and assumes the role of Thor. Jane wields the hammer throughout multiple storylines in ways that Asgardians and the Marvel universe had never seen before. This chapter will closely examine *Thor: The Goddess of Thunder* as a unique study of masculinity within superhero comics by closely analyzing the comics' use of gendered language and its attention to specific bodies. *Thor: The Goddess of Thunder* not only presents a fascinating tale of discovery and loss, but also deeply explores the creation and mediation of gender norms through Jane and Odinson's ability, or inability, to wield the hammer.

SUPER BODIES AND SUPER GENDERS:
MJOLNIR'S DISRUPTION OF MALENESS AND MASCULINITY

When beginning a discussion about gender in comic books, it is important to remember that comic book heroes and heroines have long suffered from both hyperfeminine and hypermasculine standards. Rebecca Demarest (2010) examines the extremeness of this gender ideal, stating, "Superheroes that do not have as pronounced physical sexuality are not as popular [. . . and therefore] we have no room for heroes who do not exaggerate the ideals we have and emulate." *Thor* comics have been no different. Thor has maintained his image as the epitome of masculinity throughout his tenure at Marvel, and specific objects such as plotlines and characters have exclusively served to mark him as a conventional heterosexual male. What is particularly important about *Thor: The Goddess of Thunder* is that the entire comic book series serves to undermine Demarest's claim. While Thor Odinson still exhibits rippling muscles, it is very clear through the *Unworthy Thor* comics that what he has lost is more than just his hammer.

From the plot's very beginning, the comics specifically call attention to gender politics. As the comics open, an important interaction takes place between Odin the All-Father and Freyja the All-Mother, who are the king and queen on Asgard. Whereas these roles are inherently gendered because of their respective titles, Odin and Freyja are also highly gendered as individual characters. Not surprisingly, these authorities directly clash due to a difference of personality, which can be seen in their interactions with Thor in "If He Be Worthy" (2014). At one point Odin yells at Thor Odinson, demanding to know how he lost the ability to lift Mjolnir. In response, Freyja calmly tells Odin, "Yelling at him doesn't appear to be helping, dear husband." Odin immediately tries to assert his dominance over Freyja by shouting, putting Freyja down, and verbally challenging Thor Odinson's masculinity.

Masculinity in this context follows from common representations of masculinity in comics: the male is white, heterosexual, and takes up space with pronounced muscles while acting out loudly, violently, and angrily. Yann Roblou (2012) explains that in the comic book genre "masculinity 'must be created,' thus presenting itself not so much as a given rather than a constructed dimension of the characters." In other words, characters like Odin must establish what masculinity looks like in order for the comics to question another character's masculinity (Thor's) or ascribe that masculinity to a nonconventional masculine body (Jane). Furthering Roblou's point, Judith Butler (1987) explains that:

> Gender is in no way a stable identity or locus of agency from which various acts proceed; rather, it is an identity tenuously constituted in time—an identity

instituted through *a stylized repetition of acts*. Further, gender is instituted through the stylization of the body and, hence, must be understood as the mundane way in which bodily gestures, movements, and enactments of various kinds constitute the illusion of an abiding gendered self. (900)

Applying Butler's (1987) theory to *Thor: The Goddess of Thunder,* Odin and Freyja become tools to establish the expected gender roles within the realm of this specific comic book, rather than independent characters. In this way, Odin and Freyja function to establish traditional gender performances. When Thor Odinson no longer exhibits the traits of established masculinity, crying when he can no longer pick up the hammer, he is deemed unworthy in the eyes of Odin and stripped of not only his mystical powers but also the title of Thor. As a result, he is referenced exclusively as Odinson until he regains the power to wield the hammer several years later. It is this failure of masculinity that builds Odinson's central internal conflict during his time as the Unworthy Thor.

Thor: The Goddess of Thunder shifts the focus of analysis by changing the very definition and focus of masculinity. Halberstam's (2004) analysis of action films becomes absolutely pertinent to an understanding of Thor: "Because masculinity tends to manifest as natural gender itself, the action flick, with its emphases on prosthetic extension, actually undermines the heterosexuality of the hero even as it extends his masculinity" (937). Extending on this point, Odinson is only masculine in reference to those objects surrounding him. Indeed, Odinson's masculinity only holds up as long as he possesses Mjolnir and surrounds himself with others who are subordinated by his masculinity and heterosexuality. When Odinson is no longer able to lift Mjolnir his masculinity is severely damaged, disrupting his representation in the comics as the primary pillar of Marvel masculinity.

However, as Jane is able to lift Mjolnir she symbolically begins to carry the mantel of masculinity and therefore shifts the locus of masculinity to her body. As Odinson's initial masculinity was largely characterized and reaffirmed by the props or characters he surrounded himself with—for instance Mjolnir can be seen as the prime locus of definable masculinity—then Jane must also be subjected to a similar peripheral reading of masculinity. This shift situates masculinity in a new framework by reallocating the primary container of masculinity to a different body. Halberstam's (2004) introduction reaffirms these intentions as the piece calls for texts that "begin not by subverting masculine power or taking up a position against masculine power but by turning a blind eye to conventional masculinities and refusing to engage" (936). Jane is set up to exemplify female masculinity by doing precisely this; she wields Mjolnir boldly, defiantly, and heroically in a way that resonates with the hammer so well that she is in fact more powerful than Odinson ever was.

Odinson's masculinity is thus largely disconnected from him when he loses the ability to lift Mjolnir. The comics, in turn, set up an engaging new way to see how masculinity can be played out on a body by allowing Jane Foster to pick up the hammer and wield the powers of Thor. Jane in her purely human form is a cancer-stricken wreck. She demonstrates the repercussions of chemotherapy physically, and we see her suffer through the trials of undergoing regular treatments throughout the series. This body is in huge contrast with her body when she is in control of the power of Thor. When wielding the hammer, Jane has long, flowing blonde hair reminiscent of Odinson and her body is at the peak of female physical fitness, rife with muscles but still lean, and not over sexualized while remaining curvy with a sense of sexuality. Ultimately, Jane becomes coded with both masculinity and femininity when she wields Mjolnir, thereby breaking down the binaries that equate male and female with masculine and feminine.

However, before diving deeper into an analysis of Jane's embodiment of masculinity, and how this masculinity is played out in the comics, it is important to spend more time with Mjolnir as an object and character in this saga as well. If the persona of Thor can be separated from a particular body altogether based on who can wield Mjolnir then the identity of Thor must lie in some ways with the hammer. Given that Mjolnir is transferable between bodies, the hammer itself must, to a certain extent, encompass both masculine and feminine elements. Demarest (2010) creates a link between gender and superpowers that is useful in considering Mjolnir as a gendered object. According to Demarest (2010), "Men have implied powers, yet women don't, and the women's powers were often gifted to them by males." Demarest (2010) goes on to explain, writing in relation to the X-Men comics,

> The females on the team have powers such as telekinesis, weather control, matter phasing (where she can walk through solid matter), and a super sonic voice to name a few. These are what I like to call defensive powers, they are not designed to take the offensive, but to react to an attack with a force field, etc. The men on the team have burning lasers that shoot from their eyes, an Adamantium skeleton and super healing, super strength, an armored shell, etc., all designed for the offensive, to take the initiative and attack.

Even prior to Jane's lifting the hammer, Odinson encompasses powers that are both masculine and feminine by Demarest's (2010) definitions. Whereas Thor Odinson is super strong and trained in the arts of war, he is also able to control elements of the weather—notably thunder and lightning—and fly, both of which could be considered "defensive" powers because they are not designed to take offensive action. This mixture of powers imply that Mjolnir is not an inherently gendered object, but is instead specifically ascribed by choice as Thor's accessory of masculinity, most noticeably because of its phallic nature.

Mjolnir's powers do not change when Jane assumes the role of Thor. In fact, Jane is able to control the powers better than Odinson. The extent of Jane's abilities clearly concerns many characters at the beginning of the comics, but the characters come to accept this power following the defeat of the Destroyer. Among them, Odinson is willing to accept that the hammer chose her to be its wielder instead of him, which is a bold move for a character whose entire identity and masculinity has been reaffirmed by Mjolnir's presence. Whereas other comic book characters and conventions have played with gender norms, *Thor: The Goddess of Thunder* quite possibly changes the way we see the gender norm altogether. It does so by disrupting Thor as an extremely gendered Norse myth throughout history, thereby calling into question normative gender depictions at large.

Mjolnir's representation as a bigendered object in the comics is supported by Halberstam's (2004) discussion of female masculinity as he explores the construction of masculinity by considering masculinity as a performance that can be appropriated by both men and women. Halberstam (2004) argues that "Many 'heroic masculinities' depend absolutely on the subordination of alternative masculinities[. . . .] If what we call dominant masculinity appears to be a naturalized relation between maleness and power, then it makes little sense to examine men for the contours of that masculinity's social construction" (935). Halberstam's (2004) examination of masculinity explains that masculinity is not in any way inherently connected to maleness but can only by defined by those things that are or are not socially considered masculine. As briefly described in the introduction of this chapter, Halberstam's (2004) method of analysis calls upon an examination of gender-coded objects that are related to a central point or person that is considered masculine. "Female masculinities are framed as the rejected scraps of dominant masculinity which actually affords us a glimpse of how masculinity is constructed as masculinity" (Halberstam 2004, 935). These are the "scraps" of masculinity that allow for such a unique reading of masculinity, Thor, Mjolnir, and *The Goddess of Thunder.*

Jane's narrative subverts the traditional female narrative through how she came to possess masculinity and how she wields it. Whereas Odinson relied on other characters to bolster his masculinity, Jane's masculinity is convoluted because she is the main female character in the series—a complication that is largely evident when she faces the Ice Giants. As Odinson rejects Jane's possession of Mjolnir, Jane uses Mjolnir to single-handedly bring down the Ice Giants with one throw—a feat that Odinson was unable to complete with or without Mjolnir. In the panel on "Thor vs. Thor" (2014), Odinson looks up in awe as Mjolnir zooms around the page, repeatedly striking the Ice Giants, exclaiming "Odin's beard . . . I have never seen it . . . do that before." In this moment, Odinson admires with defeat that the hammer works better for a woman than it ever did for him, a shocking admission given how much he grieved over its loss, and the phallic symbolism Mjolnir plays in reaffirming Odinson's masculinity.

LINGUISTICS AND GENDER: SPEAKING ASGARDIAN YET THINKING FEMALE

In contrast with Odinson's desperate attempt to maintain his masculinity, Jane performs in specific gendered ways, which allows her to maintain both masculine and feminine performances while she is Thor. When Jane experiences the transformation for the first time, the difference between her assumed persona as Thor and her thoughts are markedly different linguistically. When first working through the fact that she is able to lift the hammer in "If He Be Worthy" (2014), her speech and thoughts are separated by font so the reader can easily see the difference. When Jane thinks her thoughts are in a feminine dialect: "I can't believe I am holding Mjolnir! Does that make me . . ." When Jane speaks however, the dialect is much different: "Nay, no time for questions. Migard is in peril." It is clear that her thoughts reflect her human self, whereas her actual speech is affected by the sudden appropriation of Asgardian abilities, powers, and customs. This difference in speech and thought continues throughout the comics and is more noticeable when she comes face to face with Odinson because of their history as a couple. For instance, in "Thor vs. Thor" (2014), following the first major battle that Odinson and Jane fight together, Odinson remarks, "You have brought new life to that hammer. Whoever you are . . . you are correct. It has chosen you." In response Jane thinks, "He's so sad. I hate to see him like this. I just want to hug him. Do superheroes hug each other?" This moment demonstrates that there is a gender status quo within the comics: when Odinson and Jane are in close proximity, the characters must abide by traditional gender roles in order to reinstate the fact that gender is an active construct of the comics. Jane's overly feminine thoughts reaffirm that she is, in fact, a woman in spite of her ability to wield Mjolnir. By allowing Jane more feminine thoughts, she is able to control a verbally masculine discourse, which in turn allows her to wield Mjolnir at a more advanced level than Odinson.

Whereas her actions are largely a mixture of gendered performances, she maintains the agency to be both masculine and feminine in spite of the performances and roles other characters try to ascribe to her. This constitutes her possession of masculinity inherent and not dependent on characters or objects surrounding her. The biggest threat to this agency is her human form and her interactions with Odinson. In both these cases, she is ascribed a solely feminine role. When Jane is in her human form, she is clearly extremely sick. Jane wears a scarf wrapped on her head to hide her baldness and her face is sunken in, advertising the chemotherapy's side effects. Contrasting greatly with Jane's appearance when she is Thor, Jane's skeletal and asexualized human appearance negates nearly all conventional gender performances.

In regard to Jane and Odinson's relationship, the comics make it clear that Jane and Odinson's heterosexuality are heavily dependent on one another. This relationship specifically labels both Jane and Odinson within stereotypical gender bounds, in spite of her asexualized appearance. This appearance functions to allow a simultaneously masculine and feminine character, similar to her ability to wield Mjolnir. While she is Thor, Jane's masculinity is bolstered because of her ability to wield Mjolnir and therefore her femininity must also be bolstered to maintain an acceptable and believable feminine character. While she is in her human form, neither her masculinity nor femininity is exaggerated. In turn, she maintains a gender balance while in this form because she is neither overly masculine nor feminine. Jane's possession of masculine and feminine qualities then ascribes her a unique agency that does not come from what others around her prescribe for her, but from her battle with cancer and ability to wield Mjolnir. In short, her gender is related to the way she interacts with two different objects in the comics: Odinson and the hammer.

As Odinson and Jane both assume the role of Thor the reader is forced to understand masculinity and gender in a new way. While we are accustomed to understanding gender as performed by a person, the comics disrupt that understanding by prescribing masculinity to an object through Jane's use of language. Maleness is linguistically mapped onto the hammer because of the inscription on the hammer itself: "Whomsoever holds this hammer if he be worthy shall possess the power of . . . Thor." The use of a specific pronoun designates that Mjolnir is to be wielded by a particular and specific gender: he. This instance of specific pronoun on the hammer not only harkens back to the original mythology of the hammer itself, but also poses an interesting linguistic conundrum. The pronoun "he" has been used historically to indicate either sex. However, in this case because Jane is able to pick up the hammer, she transgresses the direct order of the verbiage of the power of the hammer, which we can better understand through Luce Irigaray's (2004) concept of mimicry. Irigaray (2004) argues that if we submit women to common stereotypes, we will be able to critique the discourse in which these stereotypes come from and thus create a separation between feminine and masculine discourse. Irigaray (2004) claims "One must assume the feminine role deliberately[. . . .] To play with mimesis is thus, for a woman, to try to recover the place of her exploitation by discourse, without allowing herself to be simply reduced to it" (795). In other words, in order to engage with mimicry for analysis and critique, one must first embrace stereotypes and use those stereotypes to critique the larger system. Juxtaposing Irigaray's (2004) theory with the verbiage of the hammer poses an interesting reading of the problem at hand. As Jane lifts the hammer, she is subjected to the common stereotypes associated with ideal masculinity, such as the phallic nature of the hammer and the strength her body gains just by picking the hammer up. As a woman, she mimics these stereotypes and overcomes them by using the hammer better than her male counterpart, critiquing the larger system by proving it can be made better. Her actions, all in all, are in this way similar to the theoretical act of mimesis. Thus, because she is able to lift the hammer and wield it—and wield it better than a man—her abilities are remarkably transgressive. As Jane lifts Mjolnir from the surface of the moon, it can only be understood that whoever can lift Mjolnir is able to wield the ultimate form of masculinity—regardless of characteristics that would otherwise be crucial to typical understandings of gender binaries. Juxtaposing the concept that Jane is able to become Thor, with the traditional myth of Thor as a mythical male, renders turmoil not only in the narrative's universe but also in most Western understandings of masculinity and mythical figures as we know them.

CONTEMPORARY REPERCUSSIONS: THE PROGRESSIVE-YET-REGRESSIVE DILEMMA

Considering the narrative arc of *Thor: The Goddess of Thunder* at large, the comics series does a lot with gender and complicates how masculinity is mapped onto various bodies. But with a narrative like this, it is hard not to get equally excited about the steps it makes forward as well as frustrated with the steps it has to take backwards in order to be accepted by a larger, contemporary audience. Jane is progressive because she is able to fluidly maintain both hypermasculinity and hyperfemininity as Thor. Jane's character in this story arc seeks to tackle exhaustive stereotypes that have been faced by women for centuries by showing that women are capable of wielding power and fighting just as well—if not better—than men. In addition, *Thor: The Goddess of Thunder*'s adaptation of one of the most commonly known mythological characters and superheroes demonstrates a unique understanding of that character and his hammer, as well as reveals that Mjolnir is much more than a hilariously phallic symbol of masculinity. However, close analysis of Jane's entire run as Thor reveals that there are some gender stereotypes we have yet to step away from, as exemplified by her relationship with Odinson and the difference in her speech and thought patterns when she is Thor.

Odinson and Jane are certainly not the first to be simultaneously progressive and regressive. Sharon Zechowski and Caryn E. Neuman (2014) examine Wonder Woman as a mutually progressive and regressive character. They explain that "although her mission is to combat the evils of patriarchy, Wonder Woman is also its ultimate projection of female perfection. As such, it is this idealization of her femininity that weakens her status as a progressive female character" (Zechowski and Neuman 2014). By creating, and unfortunately reinforcing, a world that follows conventional gender constructs, progressive and transgressive elements can be contained within comics by creating and managing a status quo. In other words, regressive elements are required in comics in order for comics to be believable and accepted by the larger audience as cannon. These regressive elements must coincide with overtly progressive elements in order to remain within a realistic realm. For instance, if Odinson was suddenly overly emotional and completely lost his desire to fight when Jane picked up the hammer and assumed the mantel of Thor, the consistency of the character in the canonical Marvel universe would be lost and the story's popularity would plummet. Thus, finding a balance between the ends of the gender spectrum allows for progressive elements to exist within the series. By constructing such clear gender roles at the beginning of the comics through Odin and Freyja, the status quo is made clear: whereas women are able to be free thinking and clever, women are still subjugated to men in positions of power. Interestingly enough, the story arc of the comics work to unravel this gendered system by foiling Odin and Freyja with Odinson and Jane.

In spite of how stereotypes must be used in order to build a status quo, by the end of *Thor: The Goddess of Thunder* it is ultimately Jane who remains Thor while Odinson accepts that he is unworthy. While in a future story arc she eventually has to relinquish her role as Thor, enabling Odinson to regain it, Jane's ability to wield Mjolnir better than Odinson forces him, and the reader, to deal with the fact a woman has the ability to wield a symbolically masculine object better than a man. The notion that gender is mapped onto the body by how masculinity is used to obtain agency instead of by sex or social expectations makes Jane's character incredibly progressive because she can fight with and sustain an ultimate instantiation of masculinity, even if that masculinity is literally tearing her body apart faster than cancer can.

Jane impressively retains her role as Thor for quite some time. Over the course of the next several years, Jane would retain the role of Thor in *Secret Wars, All-New All-Different Marvel,* and *All-New All-Different Avengers,* fighting through the Battleworld and eventually becoming a part of the Avengers. However, Jane's health takes a turn for the worst in "The Death of the Mighty Thor" (2018). In turn, when she transforms, the transformation negates her chemotherapy sessions, worsening her physical health each time she transforms back into a human. Upon collapsing after a transformation, Jane finds herself bedridden as her friends realize the direness of her situation: "Being Thor is going to kill you, Jane Foster, surer than Malekith ever will." Clearly mourning the loss of her power, Jane must watch her friends leave to defend Asgard from a terrible beast called the Mangog while she remains on Earth bedridden and under Doctor Strange's care.

During her time in the hospital, the reader catches glimpses into Jane's past and Odinson's role in it, images that overlap with the fight happening on Asgard. The conflation of the images between Jane's memories and the fight on Asgard paint a clear picture of Jane's struggle. As Jane's friends lose to the Mangog, her body slowly loses to cancer. She must either choose to save her friends and Asgard, or to save her own life. Jane's inability to use Mjolnir to save Asgard is not so different from Odinson's reaction when he could no longer lift the hammer: Jane is bedridden and forlornly reflects on her past struggles as she mourns her loss of power—a moment that is highly reminiscent of Odinson's monologue describing his struggle with losing the hammer at the beginning of the story arc. The result of these moments thrusts both heroes to accept their fate and push on to the next chapter of the monomythic tale they have been written into: "I would have beaten you, you little cancerous sons of bitches." She becomes Thor one more time while realizing that this will be the last transformation her body will be capable of handling. Later in battle, she realizes that the only way to defeat Mangog is to throw Mjolnir into the sun, effectively defeating the monster, but also shattering the magical hammer. Facing the loss of Mjolnir, Jane and Odinson are forced to consider an identity without the power of the hammer. Whereas Odinson must surrender this identity and create a new identity in the hammer's absence as the Unworthy Thor, Jane sacrifices the last of her life force not only to save her friends, but also to feel Mjolnir's power one more time.

Symbolically her fight with the Mangog signals a final gender struggle in Jane's run as Thor, as it is certainly no coincidence that the villain she must fight literally has the word "man" in it. However, this power struggle becomes less about her ability to wield masculinity and more about her transition back to a character that primarily adopts femininity. For the first time, Jane reveals why she risks her life to become Thor and fight in "Sundown" (2018): "I . . . die for . . . I die for love, Mangog." It is Jane's choice to ultimately die for love that both makes her a hero, but also makes her outstandingly feminine, as love is an overwhelmingly traditional trope that invokes acts of women's aggression.

During the fighting sequence between Jane and the Mangog, the other male characters spend their time either admiring her physical fighting skills or remarking that upon her death they plan to take Mjolnir. Odinson fights alongside her, scolding her choice to sacrifice her life in order to save Asgard and to throw Mjolnir into the sun. Odinson's masculinity is so conflicted that for a moment he is more upset that Mjolnir was thrown into the sun than Jane's imminent demise following her final transformation. However, as he realizes the duality of her sacrifice—the sacrifice of both Mjolnir and her life—he begins to mourn her decision more emotionally. The gender struggle that Jane's time spent as Thor ultimately comes to an end following her death and revival. Ultimately, she transforms back into a more feminine character and passes the mantle of Thor back to Odinson by giving him the final shard of Mjolnir to hold, which he is now able to lift, signaling that he is once again worthy.

Whereas it is unsurprising that she chooses to transform, save Asgard, die a heroic death, and be brought back from the dead given comic book conventions; her choice in "Mighty Thor #706" to permanently resign as Thor and hand Odinson the last remaining shard of Mjolnir was a surprise given how progressive this character had been for several years. Jane can still be considered progressive for her sacrifice and for teaching the gods humility, but her story arc from *Thor: The Goddess of Thunder* to her time in *The Mighty Thor* ultimately falls into the mold of Sandra J. Lindow's (2014) female monomyth: while Jane was able to save Asgard, she was forced to give up Mjolnir and return to less than ideal circumstances given the gravity of her cancer. Both Odinson and Jane are deeply impacted by the loss of the hammer and mourn its loss together. However, Jane is now subjugated once again to be Odinson's sidekick and supporter instead of the active character she was as Thor, regressing her role in the Marvel comic book universe back to the margins.

Jane Foster's time as Thor certainly surprised comic book fans and marked a unique moment in comic book history because of its attempt to challenge gender norms by gender bending a character derived from myth. While a close reading shows that female characters are still forced to abide by heteronormative expectations in order to be progressive, this comic book series offers a look at masculinity by using a female body, something that most scholars like Winnberg and colleagues (2008) argue does not happen enough. *Thor: The Goddess of Thunder* specifically highlights the gender political element in the story by creating a story arc that focuses around Odinson's loss of masculinity and redefines masculinity in relation to Mjolnir. This story arc allows us to examine how masculinity can be mapped onto both male and female bodies through both Butler's (1988) understanding of gender and the body, and Halberstam's (2004) understanding of female masculinity because of the relationship between Odinson, Jane, and Mjolnir.

Jane certainly marks a step forward for specific representations of gender by considering how an object prescribes gender to a specific body as well as how performances and bodies mediate that gender through the text's use of specific language. Given how much this story arc accomplished, it is a disappointment that the arc itself folded Jane back into the female monomyth. In the end, Jane's cancer plays a large role in her ability to wield femininity as a human and her ability to wield hypermasculinity as Thor, but it is also the only reason she must give up that hypermasculinity. Ultimately, *Thor: The Goddess of Thunder* offers an opportunity to analyze masculinity through the use of a female body, which is incredibly important not only for comics, but for masculinity at large.

REFERENCES

[Aaron, Jason (w) and Russell Dauterman (pi).] 2014. "If He Be Worthy." In *Thor: The Goddess of Thunder*. Marvel [Marvel Comics].

[Aaron, Jason (w) and Russell Dauterman (pi).] 2018. "The Death of the Mighty Thor." In *Mighty Thor*. Marvel [Marvel Comics].

[Aaron, Jason (w) and Mike Deodato Jr (pi).] 2014. "The One Who Watches." In the *Original Sin*. Marvel [Marvel Comics].

[Aaron, Jason (w) and Russell Dauterman (pi).] 2018. "Sundown." In *Mighty Thor*. Marvel [Marvel Comics].

[Aaron, Jason (w) and Russell Dauterman (pi).] 2014. "Thor vs. Thor." In *Thor: The Goddess of Thunder*. Marvel [Marvel Comics].

Butler, Judith. 1987. "Sex and Gender in Simone De Beauvoir's 'Second Sex'." *Yale French Studies* 72, 35–49.

Butler, Judith. 1988. "Performative Acts and Gender Constitution: An Essay in Phenomenology and Feminist Theory." *Theatre Journal* 40, no. 4, 519–31. www.jstor.org/stable/3207893.

Demarest, Rebecca A. 2010. "Superheroes, Superpowers, and Sexuality," *Inquiries Journal/Student Pulse* 2. http://www.inquiriesjournal.com/a?id=312.

Halberstam, Jack. 2004. "Female Masculinity." In *Literary Theory: An Anthology*, 935–56. Hoboken, New Jersey: Blackwell Publishing.

Irigaray, Luce. 2004. "The Power of Discourse and the Subordination of the Feminine." In *Literary Theory: An Anthology*. 795–811. Edited by Julie Rivkin and Michael Ryan. Hoboken, New Jersey: Blackwell Publishing.

Lindow, Sandra J. 2014. "To Heck with the Village: Fantastic Heroes, Journey and Return." In *Heroines of Comic Books and Literature*. 3–15. Edited by Maja Bajac-Carter, Norma Jones, and Bob Batchelor. Lanham, MD: Rowman & Littlefield.

Roblou, Yann. 2012. "Complex Masculinities: The Superhero in Modern American Movies." In *Culture, Society & Masculinities*, no. 1, 76–91. EBSCOhost, DOI: 10.3149/CSM.0401.76.

Secret Wars II. 2015. Marvel [Marvel Comics].

The Unworthy Thor. 2016–2017. Marvel [Marvel Comics].

Thor. 2011. Directed by Kenneth Branagh. Performed by Chris Hemsworth. USA: Paramount, Film.

Winnberg, Jakob, Anna Fåhraeus, and AnnKatrin Jonsson, 2008. Humanistiska fakulteten, Göteborgs universitet, Gothenburg University, Faculty of Arts, Engelska institutionen, and Department of English. "Introduction: Female Masculinity or Textual Masculinity," *Nordic Journal of English Studies* 7, no. 1: 1.

Zechowski, Sharon, and Caryn E. Neuman. 2014. "The Mother of All Superheroes: Idealizations of Femininity in *Wonder Woman*" In *Heroines of Comic Books and Literature* 133–43. Edited by Maja Bajac-Carter, Norma Jones, and Bob Batchelor. Lanham, MD: Rowman & Littlefield.

Chapter Seven

Poisoning Masculinity

*Poison Ivy as a Counter-Narrative of
Villainy and Trauma through Representations of
Queer Love in DC's* Everyone Loves Ivy

T. J. Buttgereit, Emily Mendelson,
and J. L. Schatz

In many ways the comic book series *Everyone Loves Ivy* begins itself in the fashion of a very typical Poison Ivy story. Ivy, who is traditionally a villainous character, appears in the dreams of Bruce Wayne. She is depicted using common tropes of seduction and charm as she attempts to convince the sleeping Wayne that he is in love with her. However, Bruce quickly jumps out of bed, runs to his Batcave, and injects himself with a convenient immunization. For readers of the three-issue comics series, which was published between February and March of 2018 by DC Comics, this is their first introduction to Poison Ivy. They are told that Ivy's intentions are to take control of the minds of all humans, super or otherwise, and force them all to love her. She achieves this by poisoning plants to release chemicals that steal the will of people. Through this united love, Ivy seeks to save the world from the destructive nature of humanity and capitalist modes of production. Because this love is created as the result of seduction and charm, the opening issue of the comics series seems to play a part in a long tradition within comic books for male authors and viewers to make Poison Ivy the subject of sexual fantasy. Every aspect of Poison Ivy has been created by men for men, producing and consuming Ivy as an object of pleasure. Her role as a femme fatale serves to make her an enticing object of consumption for male readers, and her sympathetic and often traumatic backstory makes her a perfect candidate for masculine tales of saviorhood.

Dorian Dawes (2018) traces the history of this trope through Ivy's appearances in media such as the *Batman and Robin* animated series and the live action *Batman and Robin* movies. Throughout these examples, Ivy is often portrayed as a passive object of sexuality who perpetrates numerous harmful tropes and stereotypes, the most prominent among them being the femme fatale. It cannot be denied that this tradition lingers within the pages of *Everyone Loves Ivy*. However, this essay serves to open the possibility of rearticulating Poison Ivy beyond the character's fetishistic masculine origins. We argue instead that the series can be interpreted in a way that allows the reader to deal with questions of queerness, trauma, and Poison Ivy's liminal relationship to the hero/villain binary. In short, Ivy is an important site for interrogating heteronormative masculinity, and can be used to display alternate forms of healing that can take place within queer moments of intimacy.

As such, this paper serves to connect the issues of gender and queerness to illustrate how they intersect and manifest within the character of Poison Ivy and her identity as a supervillain. In many ways, Poison Ivy has been forced to drift through these categories throughout her existence as a character. The unease in which her own personal identity is displayed within *Everyone Loves Ivy* demonstrates the negative consequences that come from the impossibility for Ivy to articulate herself outside of the male gaze. This is true both in the world of the comics and the world of the reader. In the face of the identity-based trauma Poison Ivy is subject to, we explore the relationship between herself and Harley Quinn to understand the ways characters in comic books can grapple with moments of lost identity.

Poison Ivy was first introduced in *Batman* #181 (1966) as Dr. Lillian Rose in a comic titled "Beware of Poison Ivy" (Mackenzie and Walker 2016). In this issue, Ivy is introduced through one of her two most historically prominent character traits, her sexuality. Integral to Poison Ivy's character has been her role as, what John-David Checkett (2001) describes, a femme fatale. A femme fatale is a feminine character that uses her sexuality and skills of seduction against her enemies, such as the mythical creature the siren (Checkett 2001, 98). According to him "Pamela Lillian Isly was rendered toxic by her plants, which, while not causing her any long-term damage personally, endowed her with the ability to kill with a kiss—or merely turn men into willing slaves, depending on which chemicals she chooses to emit" (Checkett 2001, 117). This describes Ivy's appearance and behavior as essential to her abilities, while cementing her sexuality as a core component of her character and her identity as a villain. However, as we will explore later, *Everyone Loves Ivy* and Poison Ivy's relationship to queerness complicate this reading of Ivy as a woman who only sees sex and emotions as weapons. Particularly in issue one of the series, Ivy expresses her desire to create a loving world. This world is one where humans appreciate and care for the Earth rather than try to destroy it. Ivy's affection and intimate relationship with nature is a queer one because it defies the masculine and capitalist desire to see nature as an object to be used and consumed (Checkett 2001, 21). Therefore, rather than cementing sexist tropes of seduction and women using sex as a weapon, Ivy's relationship to sexuality can instead be read as a queer orientation that challenges capitalist norms of domination.

Keeping with the discussion of Ivy's character as an ecofeminist symbol, in 1986 Poison Ivy experienced a transformation in character and identity through the work of Neil Gaiman and Mike Dringenberg in DC's *Secret Origins* series (Mackenzie and Walker 2016). This change in character focused around the development of another core aspect of the modern Poison Ivy, her role as an ecoterrorist (Mackenzie and Walker 2016). Now an anti-social scientist who found more comfort in nature than human communities, the character of Poison Ivy became attached to the social issue of climate change and environmental destruction. Although Ivy's motivation to combat climate change was a way for readers to sympathize with her, her placement as a villain in the comics was still used to alienate readers. This intentionally prevents readers from identifying with Ivy as a character and reflects the way capitalist power relations seeks to demonize causes of ecological protection and valorize corporate power. This shift serves to paint Ivy in the light of a good-hearted but misguided character, whose methods betray her intentions—much as news media painted the picture of the Earth Liberation Front against the corporate victims, which they were fighting to save the environment (Pickering 2002). While the trope of Ivy as "the villain" in her stories is sometimes inconsistent, key aspects of her character have included her dedication to ecoterrorism and seductive abilities. However, there are other suppressed aspects of Ivy's personality that make their way into comics such as *Everyone Loves Ivy*. Therefore, it is important to explore Ivy as a queer feminist woman within the world of DC Comics, and question why it is that this view of her is often suppressed within mainstream discussions of her character.

FEMINISM AND QUEERNESS IN THE SUPERHERO/VILLAIN FIGURE

The question of how women are represented in comic book stories has become an increasingly prominent issue in recent years. Female characters such as Black Widow, Wonder Woman, and Captain Marvel have become popular fan favorites within the Marvel Cinematic Universe. Beyond the simple representation of women characters in mainstream movies, Valentina Cardo and Neal Curtis (2018) argue that the culture of comics has been greatly changed and influenced by the ideas of third-wave feminism. Not only has the quantity of representation increased—both among fictional characters and artists employed by companies such as Marvel and DC—but the quality of representation has shifted in many ways to subvert common misogynistic stereotypes in order to introduce feminist principles consistent with the ideals of modern feminism (Cardo and Curtis 2018). Cardo and Curtis (2018) highlight examples such as America Chavez and Kamala Kahn (Ms. Marvel), who both serve as important representations of character lives that are lived at the intersection of race, gender, class, sexuality, and religious affiliation.

In analyzing the issue of feminine representation in comic books, Ingrid Marie Fretheim (2017) isolates major categories such as body image, origin story, and the character's relationship to a hero identity as important to understand representation. Fretheim (2017) focuses her analysis on the superheroes Wonder Woman, She Hulk, and Black Widow to provide a more critical perspective on the inclusion of female characters in comics. She notes that while male superheroes tend to have realistically masculine physical features, "for female superheroes, however, a hyperfeminine exterior has become the rule, and in contrast to the hypermasculine physique, the hyperfeminine body is not compatible with a realistic superhero muscle mass" (Fretheim 2017, 77). The normalization of hyperfeminine features among popular female superheroes serves to create a binary between physically attractive role models and those female characters who become social outcasts because they don't meet the standards of Western feminine beauty. As a result, a tension exists between the desire to celebrate comics that introduce and represent diverse and modern women characters, while also recognizing the pervasive ways these characters are objectified to fulfill masculine fantasies. This tension can be seen within the scope of this paper. While we argue that *Everyone Loves Ivy* can offer positive representations of queer women, this interpretation should not be used to purify every aspect of these comics and of the character Poison Ivy in all her iterations. Therefore, there is a clear need for caution when one attempts to speak about the sheer presence of women in comics as an act against toxic masculinity because it is equally important to attend to how these characters are deployed within the stories and the comics industry at large.

By using the term toxic masculinity, we mean to point to the ways that communities and genres of fiction, such as comics, often participate in exclusive and harmful tropes and practices regarding women and issues of sexuality. Blodgett and Salter (2017) specifically discuss this phenomenon regarding the sexualization of feminine characters and how that relates to larger "geek culture." They argue that because women in comics have primarily been displayed as sex objects whose physical appearance has been emphasized as their dominant character traits, it becomes difficult for the "Geek Girl" identity to formulate itself. Because the idea of being a "geek" and being "sexy" are rarely associated together, women who attempt to participate in geek culture are often seen as fake or disingenuous in their intentions

(Blodgett and Salter 2017, 104). Therefore, there are clear consequences to the constant sexualization of women characters in the genre of superhero comics. In short, as it teaches male audiences to internalize tropes of sexy women, which then get weaponized against women who try to participate in comic book culture. This issue of sexualization is evidentially true with the character of Poison Ivy, who as previously mentioned, has been stereotypically portrayed as the seductive object of male fantasy, one with some traumatic past and naive ideals that make her perfect for a paternalistic redemption arc. Despite Poison Ivy providing an important example in the discussion of both representation of identity and the existence of tropes in comics, she is rarely mentioned in either Cardo and Curtis's (2018) or Fretheim's work (2017).

Poison Ivy is not just represented as a woman in comic books. Rather, she is also often portrayed as a queer woman. Both Poison Ivy and Harley Quinn have been of growing importance to queer representation in this genre as more and more comics have been published exploring their relationship. However, these are not the only two characters in DC Comics that have been used to represent issues of queerness. For example, there is a long history of the discussion of the sexuality of characters such as Batman's sidekick Robin and his superhero ally Bat-Woman (Gilroy 2015). The former has a history of being discussed in context of Robin's homosocial relationship to his older mentor Batman, while the latter has often represented a more masculine and "butch" interpretation of a superheroine (Gilroy 2015). These subtextual connections to queerness however, especially in the context of Harley Quinn and Poison Ivy, have been a subject of consistent criticism. These two characters have continuously displayed a subtle and contextual romantic interest, although for a while it remained unofficial (Glover 2017). That changed, however, in *Harley Quinn* #25 (2017) when Ivy and Quinn share a passionate and open kiss for both the audience and characters in the universe, who have gathered for a party, to see (Glover 2017). This moment proves important for queer representation in comics because it sheds a light on a painful history of erasure and hidden gestures that have long marked their relationship (Glover 2017). However, as the name of comic books suggests, Harley Quinn is more often the focus of these discussions around queerness than Poison Ivy. Now a reformed villain who has castaway her long association with the Joker, Harley Quinn's relationship with Ivy is often viewed as a turning point in her character development. The effect of this turning point in relationship to Poison Ivy's character, however, is a more neglected subject of critical theory. The differences in the portrayal of their participation in a queer relationship may be due to their differing positions as a hero and villain.

Within the superhero genre, there is rarely a focus on the importance of inclusion and diversity within the realm of the supervillain. In fact, as Lee Easton (2013) points out, within mainstream superhero movies, the role of the villain has primarily been occupied by men. Despite a focus on queer representations among protagonists and heroes within the comic universe, it may be intuitive to see how queerness is commonly thematically embodied by the villain of the story. When comparing a male villain to a male hero, Easton (2013) argues that "if the superhero provides his spectators with a handy checklist of 'what makes a man a man' then the villain presents the audience with an offsetting guide to 'what makes a man unmanly'" (39). Because the villain is unable to properly perform the moral principles of masculinity, they are thus destined to be thwarted by their righteous counterpart. Here, we see the role of the villain deeply entangled with queerness' relationship to society, through deviance, disruption, and failure (Easton 2013). The villain only succeeds in defeat, as his purpose within the narrative is to ultimately reaffirm the victory of the civilized social order, which is represented by the hero. Using the work of Edelman, Easton (2013) argues that it is supervillains' resistance and desire to destroy the bright future society imagines for itself that cast them in the role of the threatening queer outsider. Characters like the Joker not only represent an antagonism to morals that society is meant to hold dear, but they also threaten humanity's hopes and aspirations for a better world (Easton 2013). This notion of the hero saving the future can be seen throughout numerous Batman comics and stories, where the protagonist interacts with and ultimately saves children at multiple points throughout the story. Joker, on the other hand, interacts with very few people at all. The audience rarely sees him speak to anyone outside threats of violence, and never in a heroic or caring way. By not establishing personal relationships, the Joker is portrayed as an irredeemable character who is nothing but dangerous to society.

While the above understanding of queerness within the narrative of comics appears reasonable when applied to male villains, we argue that rather than represent feminine traits, the emotionless and irredeemable male villain is placed in a frame of hypermasculinity. Whereas heroes such as Batman and Superman are represented as having trauma they need to overcome (loss of family or homeland), male villains represent an expulsion or lack of these emotional connections. However, female villains are represented quite differently. For women in comics, there is almost always a narrative of victimhood and the possibility of redemption. While the Joker is presented as the moral antithesis to society with no real redeeming qualities, Harley Quinn is represented as a misguided victim of the Joker's manipulation. She is often absolved for her evil past because her crimes are an extension of Joker's and not her own. This view can be seen through the eyes of Batman in the video game *Arkham City*. Within Batman's psychological profile of Quinn, he says, "As an Arkham Asylum psychiatrist assigned to treat the Joker, Doctor Harleen Quinzel instead became obsessively fixated on her patient, believing herself to be in love with him[. . . .] Because of his cruel and mercurial nature this in some ways makes her just another one of his victims, albeit a very dangerous one" (2011). By labeling Harley Quinn as "just another one of his victims," Batman robs Quinn of any agency or individual responsibility. Therefore, Harley Quinn's crimes are seen merely as an extension of the Joker, making it impossible for her identity as a villain to be formed outside of her male counterpart.

Another character whose identity as a villain is impacted by her gender is Poison Ivy. Ivy is never portrayed as an irrational hater of society such as the Joker. Rather, as mentioned before, she is portrayed as a passionate eco-terrorist who seeks to help the downtrodden but does so in the wrong ways. Because of the trauma and harm that men inflict on her, Ivy has a strong hatred toward men. This hatred, however, is created to elicit sympathy in a way that is meant to make Ivy redeemable and likeable in the mind of the audience (Checkett 2001, 151). This is unlike other justifications for villain-ous hatred, as it uniquely humanizes Ivy into almost being a hero if only she used different means to promote her ecojustice. At the point where Ivy is avenging harm and cruelty that men have done to her, her relationship to villainy becomes increasingly unclear. It appears that neither an analysis of the hero or villain identity is sufficient to theorize Poison Ivy's position as a queer woman within comics because neither fully grasps nor accounts for her actions and character.

QUEER TRAUMA, MEMORY, AND MOTIVATION

With the failure of both the hero and villain identity to accurately depict and capture Poison Ivy's relationship to gender and queerness, we instead suggest that Poison Ivy's character has been formed through a lens of trauma. Trauma must be discussed within its relationship to identity formation in comics, as well as how male heteronormative notions of trauma fail to accurately explain queer and feminine characters. In *Everyone Loves Ivy*, Ivy's relationship to trauma is connected to her character's motivations, actions, and moral justification within the comics' narrative. Throughout the series, Poison Ivy is portrayed as a somewhat unconventional villain as her motivations for her plan, such as preventing war and environmental destruction, are likely very sympathetic to the audience. However, as we have discussed, her role in this series is one that is easily categorized within the paternalistic norms of how feminine villains are portrayed. Specifically, Poison Ivy argues that she is making the world a better place by taking it over and stopping all forms of violence against humans and nature alike (King 2018a, 17). Batman expresses sympathy, but in a paternalistic tone tells Ivy that her intentions are good but that she is acting on them in supposedly incorrect ways (King

2018c, 7). Behind this trope of Ivy as a redeemable villain lies deep seated forms of trauma that are crucial to understanding her character.

As background for the *Everyone Loves Ivy* series, a few issues earlier in the run of *Batman* (2016) we see Batman's infamous villains, the Joker and the Riddler, attempt to team up to defeat him. However, these two villains had a disagreement over how they would kill Batman, specifically who would be the one to do so. As a result, a conflict between the two villains began (King 2017). This became known as "The War of the Jokes and the Riddles," and villains throughout Gotham City were forced to take sides in the conflict. Though not explicitly mentioned in the story arc itself, the final issue of *Everyone Loves Ivy* reveals that Poison Ivy in fact played a role in this war. She was either forced or convinced (it is not made entirely clear by her telling of the story) to join the Riddler's side of the war and even kill on behalf of the Riddler. This was severely traumatic for Ivy when she recounts this experience. When speaking to Catwoman, Ivy says, "So I'm weak. A poor little girl lured into a trap[. . . .] I killed five men. I wore the Riddler's signet on my arm. I fought for Riddler. As his army killed scores more," she states with a seemingly regretful tone (King 2018c, 6). Ivy attaches this to her main motivation for ensnaring the world in her plant-based spell. Ivy feels a burden to redeem herself, to prove herself a hero to a world that has consistently denied her access to that identity. Here we can see almost an existential recognition on the part of Ivy about how who she is as a character has been almost entirely scripted outside the reach of her own control.

This uncertainty and loss of identity for Ivy is the starting point upon which her character can be examined through the lens of trauma. In connecting Ivy's trauma to her identity as a queer woman, we draw upon the work of Laura S. Brown (2003) in establishing a theory of trauma as it relates to queer experiences. Particularly, Brown's (2003) reading of trauma operates under the important distinction that trauma is not just a single terrifying instance of violence, but rather a shattering or loss of expectations for the world. For Brown (2003), traumatic experiences are those which destroy the world as fair, kind, or optimistic. The coming out narrative represents an important and iconic moment of trauma within queer identity formation. Brown (2003) argues that the "act of coming out to oneself constitutes an occasion for just that sort of shattering of the beliefs in a just world. Until we know we are queer, in sexuality or gender or both, the world works in predictable ways for those of us who grow up with the good-enough experience" (57). In this way, the trauma of coming out can strongly be tied to Ivy's loss of identity and the uncertainty of being able to create a new one. In terms of the way this form of trauma effects the queer individuals in question, Brown (2003) argues, "At the very most basic level, one loses the capacity to accept that the taken for granted truths of the world are true any longer" (58).

While Poison Ivy's trauma as displayed in the story is not directly tied to her queer identity, there are many ways that it connects to the idea of a coming out moment. In the moment where Poison Ivy is being convinced to give up her control of the world, she expresses clear doubt and uncertainty not only about how she feels about others but also what she thinks about herself. The trauma experienced by Poison Ivy during the "War of the Jokes and the Riddles" is further complicated when Batman reveals that Ivy never actually killed the men she thought she had. Rather, the Riddler betrayed Ivy with a psychological trick, having killed them himself, and then subsequently framing Ivy for the murders (King 2018c, 19).

In many ways, this betrayal and psychological manipulation on behalf of the Riddler appears to resemble the relationship that both the writers and the readers of traditional Poison Ivy narratives have had with the character. Consider, as has been discussed previously, the male gaze that has historically placed Poison Ivy at the center of male-based violence and paternalism. This male gaze as discussed by Edward Avery-Natale (2013) refers to the way that representations of women serve to embody and display the fantasies of heterosexual males. In much the same way that the Riddler uses the moment of the murders to psychologically shatter and impair Ivy's self-image, writers have historically used trauma to place Poison Ivy into a male centric narrative of victimhood. This victimhood takes on both sexualized and paternalistic undertones. From the beginning of her story, Poison Ivy has been physically attractive and alluring, and her power as an independent villain was based in her ability to trick and seduce men to her gain. However, this male fantasy complicated Ivy's relationship to villainy because the role of the true and uncompromised villain had no room to accommodate a feminine woman. Rather she must represent a redeemable damsel in distress, one that can be redeemed to truly fulfill the male fantasy of an attractive yet morally pure and simple feminine object.

While it appears that this is the intended symbolic meaning of Poison Ivy's transition from misguided villain to regretful and lost hero, the narrative of *Everyone Loves Ivy* also offers an opportunity to address the issue of feminine and queer traumatization. This arrives at the very end of the comics, where Harley Quinn is brought to Poison Ivy by Batman to convince her to release the world from her control. Within this issue of the series we see how Poison Ivy's trauma is deeply connected to her uncertainty regarding her identity, and it is only by dealing with this trauma directly that Ivy can reconcile the contradictory parts of her past that prevent her from moving forward.

I'M HERE NOW, SO BE HURT WITH ME:
POISON IVY, HARLEY QUINN, AND QUEER LOVE

When Batman realizes that he was unable to defeat Poison Ivy and take away her control over the world, he sought out to free Harley Quinn, who he believed would be able to convince her to stop. Batman actively courts a fight with the Ivy-controlled Superman, winding himself up in the hospital where he is treated by a mind-controlled Quinn. While Batman distracts Ivy through speaking to Quinn, Catwoman arrives at Ivy's lair and attacks her. Catwoman succeeds in knocking Ivy unconscious providing the opportunity for Batman to startle Harley awake. With Harley removed from Ivy's control, she agrees to help Batman and the two make their way to Ivy's location in the Batmobile. Then, the scene shifts to focus on the interaction between Harley and Ivy. Harley begins the interaction with a humorous joke about Batman changing in his Batmobile. It serves as a charming and tension-breaking entrance that is fitting with Quinn's character. Poison Ivy then sees Harley and responds merely by uttering her name. Ivy's face shows surprise at Quinn's arrival and a notably relaxed tone at the sight of her companion.

"Hey Sweetie, how're you a doing?" Quinn asks with a calm smile on her face. It is interesting to note that she does not condemn or critique Ivy for her plan, nor does Quinn seem particularly concerned about the state of the world. Her attention in that moment is fully on Ivy. In a response that fits with Ivy's depiction as a traumatized villain attempting to become a hero, Ivy says, "I'm fine[. . . .] I'm saving the world." (King 2018c, 17). Here we see a radical break from Ivy's previous interactions, however, when Harley simply replies, "No Darlin', how are you doing?" This represents a powerful moment between the two; where Ivy's character is transformed from an object upon which the male author and reader's desires are placed into an embodied character whose desires and feelings are sought after and valued on their own.

This instance of asking Ivy how she feels ruptures the previous narrative of the story where she is told what she should feel, rather than asked what she feels for herself. Just before Quinn's arrival, Batman and Catwoman had incessantly told Ivy how she should feel and think about her trauma. Instead, Quinn asks her what she feels, and it is in this moment that Ivy's façade of strength and control shatters. Ivy barely manages to form a sentence as the two embrace, and Ivy shares her feelings. "They just keep saying . . . I'm hurt. . . . But I don't want to . . ." (King 2018c, 18). Here, we see the true manifestation of Ivy's trauma, which is a pain that she cannot articulate in part because she is unable to communicate her own identity outside of how others have shaped her. Harley appears unfazed by this admission and replies, "You can be hurt. It's okay. But I'm here now. We can be hurt together." The result of this interaction produces a moment of queer intimacy that offers the potential of dealing with trauma. Rather than seek an overcoming narrative to compel Ivy to transition to a hero, or to ask her to push away her pain as both masculine heroes and villains often do, Harley suggests not only accepting her own trauma but sharing it between them. This intimate moment thus redresses much of the trauma inflicted upon Ivy through the dominant masculine gaze that has been prevalent in Ivy's depiction throughout her many iterations. Ivy's relationship to queerness before this moment is obscured within her character because previously all her intimate and emotional expressions through her powers have been expressed to and for men. In this moment, we see Ivy's character temporarily escape the male focus and allow her to express genuinely queer and loving feelings toward Harley.

Some might object to the above interpretation by arguing that Batman served as a sort of heterosexual matchmaker within the setting of the comics. Within this view, Batman weaponized the feelings shared between Ivy and Quinn to reassert the male power structure that dominates the narrative of most comics. While this concern is admittedly justified, we argue that such a counterinterpretation misses a larger opportunity within the narrative. While the male gaze seems constant within the story of Poison Ivy, *Everyone Loves Ivy* presents a moment where masculinity and the male gaze are absent and instead we see a queer feminine moment of healing and acceptance. The desire for Harley to form a communal bond with Ivy presents a unique form of love and care that addresses the specific needs associated with queer trauma. In a world created so that queer women are so often forced to suffer and then receive the unwanted rehabilitation of a male savior, Ivy and Quinn offer a path to loving though trauma that seeks to neither bury nor fix queer pain, but rather use it to strengthen the bonds of intimacy and connection. In *Everyone Loves Ivy,* we are introduced to a story where the powerful male hero is in fact powerless to save the day. Instead feminine queer love takes center stage in a way that shatters the hero/villain binary that is often a product of superhero heteronormativity.

CONCLUSION

Ultimately, this chapter serves to highlight how loving through trauma, which is displayed within the conclusion of *Everyone Loves Ivy*, has the potential to disrupt the normative ways in which feminine characters such as Poison Ivy are trapped within the tropes of sexualization, vulnerability, and trauma. The femme fatale, as Poison Ivy is typically cast, makes it difficult for her character's sexuality and moral attitudes to be expressed outside of the normative male gaze. As Dorian Dawes (2018) puts it, "Turning Poison Ivy into a queer character radically alters the inherent sexist nature of the archetype. Her sexuality isn't for men. She cares little for them." While we agree that Poison Ivy's sexuality ruptures her position as a masculine sex object, we also argue that the impact of her and Quinn's relationship moves far beyond mere representations. Instead it shows how feminine queer love can be articulated in a typically masculine genre such as superhero comics. This rupturing of both the heterosexual male gaze, as well as the trope of women as objects of heterosexual fantasies, offers the potential for representation that produces better understandings of women and queerness within the cultural community of comic books.

REFERENCES

Avery-Natale, Edward. 2013. "An Analysis of Embodiment among Six Superheroes in DC Comics." *Social Thought and Research* 32, 71–106.

Batman: Arkham City, 2011. Xbox 360.

Blodgett, Bridget and Anastasia Salter. 2017. "Toxic Geek Masculinity in Media Sexism, Trolling, and Identity Policing." Cham, Switzerland: Springer Nature.

Brown, Laura S. 2003. "Sexuality, Lies, and Loss: Lesbian, Gay, and Bisexual Perspectives on Trauma." *Journal of Trauma Practice* 2, 57–68.

Cardo, Valentina and Neal Curtis. 2018. "Superhero Comics and Third Wave Feminism." *Feminist Media Studies*, 18.

Checkett, John-David. 2001. *The Green Goddess Returns: Batman's Poison Ivy as a Symbol of Emerging Ecofeminist Consciousness.* Boca Raton, FL: Florida Atlantic University.

Dawes, Dorian. 2018. "The Femme Fatale and Poison Ivy." Medium. Feb. 8, 2018. https://medium.com/@RealDorianDawes/the-femme-fatale-poison-ivy-dcfcf9ceda4a.

Easton, Lee. 2013. "Saying No to Masculinity: The Villain in the Superhero Film." *The University of British Columbia's Film Journal* 9, no. 2, 38–44.

Fretheim, Ingrid Marie. 2017. "Fantastic Feminism: Female Characters in Superhero Comic Books." DUO. Elsevier Science. September 4, 2017. https://www.duo.uio.no/handle/10852/57781.

Glover, Cameron. 2017. "Harley Quinn #25 Finally Celebrates Harley's Queerness." *GO Magazine*. August 18, 2017. http://gomag.com/article/harley-quinn-25-finally-celebrates-harleys-queerness/.

Gilroy, Andréa. 2015. "The Epistemology of the Phone Booth: The Superheroic Identity and Queer Theory in Batwoman: Elegy." English Department Website. 2015. http://www.english.ufl.edu/imagetext/archives/v8_1/gilroy/.

King, Tom. 2018a. "Everyone Loves Ivy Part One." Comic. Batman (2016). DC Comics.
———. 2018b. "Everyone Loves Ivy Part Two." Comic. Batman (2016). DC Comics.
———. 2018c. "Everyone Loves Ivy Part Three." Comic. Batman (2016). DC Comics.
———. 2017. "The War of the Jokes and Riddles." Comic. Batman (2016). DC Comics.

Mackenzie, Robert, and David Walker. 2016. "Poison Ivy—A Cycle of Life and Death." Nerdspan. January 21, 2016. http://www.nerdspan.com/author/mackenzieandwalkergmail-com/.

Pickering, Leslie. 2002. *The Earth Liberation Front: 1997–2002.* Binghamton, NY: Arissa Media Group.

Chapter Eight

The New Teen Titans for Queer Boys

Emergent Masculinities and Sentimental
Superhero Melodrama in the 1980s

Brian Johnson

I was eleven, and superhero comics were changing. Marv Wolfman and George Pérez's *The New Teen Titans* #38 was the bellwether. Its painted cover—still a novelty in 1983—immediately distinguished it from other comics on the rack. The noir palette of muddy blues, blacks, and browns seemed more suited to the cover of a crime pocketbook than a superhero comic. So too did the image: torn posters of a woman's face clinging to the wall of a burnt-out building, a trench-coated man skulking in the rubble, the cover copy teasing: "WHO IS DONNA TROY?" The trench coat wearer was barely distinguishable as Teen Titans leader Robin (Dick Grayson). Fellow Titan Wonder Girl (the Donna Troy in question) was reduced to a pictorial trace in the torn posters whose attenuated composition obscured her superhero costume. Inside were further provocations: this issue was more of a detective story than a superhero yarn. Robin was helping Wonder Girl learn the secrets of her parentage so that she could marry her nonsuperhero fiancée (college professor Terry Long), with a clear sense of her own identity. Neither "superhero" was in costume for more than a few panels and there were no supervillains or fight scenes. What this comic offered instead was a great deal of talking—and tears. Countless rereadings later, I remain astonished and moved by the earnest professions of nonromantic love between its out-of-costume male and female protagonists that differed so noticeably from the celebrated heterosexual superhero romances of the era.

To a gender-nonconforming protogay child who negotiated daily what Eve Sedgwick (1993) so aptly called "the war on effeminate boys," this comic's embrace of sentimental melodrama was revelatory (154). Already a compulsive watcher of daytime soaps and a clandestine reader of teen romance novels, I was used to seeking alternative models of masculinity (not to mention still-nebulous queer pleasures) in cultural objects addressed to women and girls. Sensitive male soap studs and paperback romance heroes may have been designed as fantasy figures for female viewers and readers, but to a boy who hated sports and preferred the company of girls, they provided early hints that "masculinity" might be a more capacious and elastic category than initially supposed. *The New Teen Titans* #38 affirmed this suspicion in a new way. Robin's chaste but loving concern for teammate Wonder Girl furnished me with an image of counterhegemonic masculinity that resonated very directly with my own experience as an effeminate older brother whose friendships with girls were powerfully sustaining. Importantly, it did so in a medium and a genre that had historically been marketed to boys. I felt uncharacteristically addressed and affirmed. Its image of a masculine hero defined not by brawn and invulnerability but by empathy and tenderness was deeply validating. In the language of queer theory, it gave unexpected credence to my "reparative" style of reading superhero comics—a style attuned to the reality that "the culture surrounding it is inadequate or inimical to its nurture" and motivated by a desire "to assemble and confer plenitude on an object that will then have resources to offer the inchoate self" (Sedgwick 2002, 149).

I begin with an anecdote about finding validation for dissonant forms of gender comportment in *The New Teen Titans* #38 because it attests to the reparative value that popular images of counterhegemonic masculinity possess in the queer life-narratives of boys who experience their social being as anomalous. The need to locate images of counterhegemonic masculinity that might serve as validating ego-ideals among queer and gender-noncomforming boys is always an urgent matter, but it was especially so in the early 1980s, a period in which a "new conservatism of heroic fantasy," epitomized by hard-bodied heroes like Rambo, was ascendant in American pop culture (Jeffords 1994, 28). In comics, this was a moment in which the comparatively subversive energies of Civil Rights-era titles like Chris Claremont's *Uncanny X-Men* (Fawaz 2016, 8–11) jostled with an emergent reactionary vogue for macho white badasses like Wolverine and the Punisher (Nelson 2004, 255). The new popularity of such tough guy antiheroes among comic book fans in the late 1970s and early 1980s anticipated the phenomenal success of Frank Miller's revisionist, brazenly homophobic *Dark Knight Returns* in 1986 (Wilde 2011, 115–17). By the early 1990s, the new toxic "hypermasculinity" became commonplace in Image Comics (Brown 1999, 33).

In the five years leading up to the reactionary gender politics of *Dark Knight Returns*, however, Wolfman and Pérez's *The New Teen Titans* was taking superhero masculinity down a different path. Cocreated and produced on a monthly basis by Wolfman and Pérez for DC Comics from 1980–1985, *The New Teen Titans* was an unexpected creative and commercial success for DC. It was also widely touted within industry and fan publications as setting a new standard of storytelling for monthly mainstream superhero comics. Such accolades were tacit validations of Wolfman and Pérez's concerted program of genre revisionism. Appropriating and transforming the action-oriented style of superhero melodrama developed at Marvel comics during the 1960s and 1970s, Wolfman and Pérez sought self-consciously to invent a new kind of superhero tale. *The New Teen Titans* was more rooted in pictorial and psychological realism than superhero comics of the preceding decade. It was also more invested in the emotional satisfactions of sentimental romance. Their models for these revisions were not other mainstream comics but relatively acclaimed middlebrow fare from neighboring genres and media: "talk" films, contemporary alternative (nonsuperhero) comics, and prime-time "quality TV" serial melodramas (Pérez 1987). As the relative cultural prestige of those intertexts and the aesthetic ambition and generic experimentalism of a story like "Who Is Donna Troy?" all suggest, Wolfman and Pérez saw their work on *The New Teen Titans* as an expansion and elevation of the aesthetic possibilities usually attributed to superhero melodrama. In all of these ways, their work on *The New Teen Titans* exemplified in the "'pulp strategy' of rebellion against the strictures of the Comics Code and the narrative and graphic limitations found in traditional mainstream comic books" (Lopes 2009, 111). By pushing past genre conventions, moreover, Wolfman and Pérez created conditions in which a particularly powerful form of counterhegemonic superhero masculinity could emerge. I call this new form "sentimental masculine melodrama" or "sentimental superhero melodrama" to distinguish it both from the *masculine melodrama* that dominated Marvel comics of the 1960s and 1970s and from the reactionary *phallic masculinities* that were consolidated by the "grim and gritty" male superheroes of the mid-eighties and their inheritors. Before turning to a detailed reading of Wolfman and Pérez's interventions into gender and genre it is necessary to glance back at the earlier gendered history of superhero melodrama to which they responded.

DUAL IDENTITIES: SUPERHERO MASCULINITIES BEFORE *THE NEW TEEN TITANS*

In the autobiographical remarks that introduce his now classic essay on superhero bodies as somatic narratives of "mastery and trauma," Scott Bukatman (2003) sums up many assumptions about the long-standing relation between superheroes, boyhood, and hegemonic masculinity: "I don't read superhero comics anymore. I'm probably not as worried about my dick as I used to be. Well, *that* isn't exactly true—but I no longer deal with it by reading about mutant musclemen and the big-titted women who love them" (2003, 48). In Bukatman's (2003) arch formulation, male superheroes are indices of adolescent insecurity as well as sites of therapeutic compensation and idealizing self-projection. They are power fantasies but also gender blueprints. They exemplify what Alan Klein (1993) once called "comic book masculinity," an ideological formation epitomized by the transformative culture of bodybuilding that Charles Atlas famously hawked in comic book ads (267). Moreover, in spite of the ambiguous homosocial ambience of superhero comics and the hero's often "dangerous" proximity to a camp aesthetic, sexualized female counterparts hover on the margins to reassure the boy reader that there is nothing queer about his fascination with mutant muscles. Thus fortified, the male superhero is free to function as a standard-bearer for the hegemonic scripts of American manhood. His generic reiteration of interlocking traits that secure this image are anatomized by Jeffrey A. Brown (1999): an unnaturally muscular and armored body; a commitment to the public sphere; an overvaluation of (usually violent) action; "invulnerability" and a consequent aversion to "feminine" intellect and emotion; an implicit privileging of whiteness; a disidentification with "animalistic" black masculinity and "feminized" queer men (26–34).

Yet, as Brown (1999) points out, even when male superheroes have historically embodied hypermasculine cultural ideals, the male superhero's celebration of phallic masculinity is never entirely free of the alternative masculinities it rejects so long as the trope of dual-identity is present. As an ego fantasy for boys who are sutured to a masculine ideal through a preliminary identification with the superhero's "weak" alter ego, the dual identity of the superhero "split[s] masculinity into two distinct camps, stressing the superhero side as the ideal to be aspired to," even as it insists that "masculinity is ultimately premised on the *inclusion* of the devalued side" (Brown 1999, 32). This structural peculiarity grants the male superhero the potentiality of being an emancipatory figure. Insofar as the superhero's dual identity ambiguously conjoins "failed" and idealized masculine scripts in order to mediate between them, it can serve as site for interrogating and complicating the very qualities of hegemonic masculinity—hardness, strength, emotional reserve, violent action—that it ostensibly valorizes. Whether or not it does so in a given instance depends not only on the idiosyncrasies of readerly desire but also on the superhero's semantic and narrative composition at that particular historical moment.

Furthermore, the history of mainstream superhero comics demonstrates the unevenness with which conventional phallic masculinity has actually dominated the gender ideology of superhero narrative and functioned as a grail for its readers. Superhero comics from the time of Superman's first appearance in 1938 until the appearance of *The Fantastic Four* in 1961 established the paradigm of "comic book masculinity" (Klein 1993, 267). But the Marvel "revolution" of the 1960s transformed this model of gender normativity in significant ways in its bid to expand the comics market by winning more college-age readers (Tucker 2017, 35). As secular myths, superhero comics had always exemplified the stark moral polarities of melodrama that Peter Brooks (1995) famously dubbed "the moral occult," which was "[t]he heightening and hyperbole, the polarized conflict, the menace and suspense [. . .] made necessary by the effort to perceive [. . .] the spiritual in a world voided by the traditional Sacred" (11). By placing greater emphasis on psychological and emotional realism of characterization, embracing the possibilities of the serialized format, and granting greater narrative determination to the tribulations of the superhero's "weak" human alter ego, Marvel deepened the superhero genre's connection to melodrama (Bainbridge 2009, 67–71).

Of particular interest to Marvel writers was the rich vein of psychologized, often explicitly Freudian, melodrama that flourished in midcentury American film and television by addressing itself to female audiences. This included the Women's Weepies of the 1940s, the "hysterical" family melodramas of Douglas Sirk, and the ubiquitous daytime soap opera, among others. As Lee Easton (2010) notes,

> This move to melodrama was hardly surprising, since in the 1950s Stan Lee, Jack Kirby and John Romita Sr., three of Marvel's chief creative movers had had to flee the Wertham-decimated superhero world, and set up shop in the field of the romance comic. [. . .] Stan Lee and the other creators took the conventions of melodrama from radio, television, and romance comics and adapted them for a male readership by infusing plenty of superheroics into what were essentially 1960s' *The Young and the Restless* episodes. (245)

Tim Nelson (2004) cites the "re-evaluation of gender role models in the wake of the Cold War" and the crisis of cultural mythology precipitated by the moral catastrophe of the Vietnam War as crucial contexts for understanding Marvel's new cathexis on weepy male heroes in the 1960s and 1970s (251–52). The famous Vision story in *Avengers* #58 (1968), "Even an Android Can Cry," is a case in point. As that issue demonstrates, all the family conflict, transgressive desire, private suffering, psychological disturbance, violent reversals, unwelcome revelations, and cathartic releases of soap opera were fair game for Marvel superhero stories in 1968.

Significantly, however, the generic hybridization at work in Marvel melodrama involved more than just attaching standard soap opera woes to the superhero's human alter ego and his open-ended narrative. The recursive *Frankenstein*-inspired Oedipal drama of murderous progeny, filial rebellion, and familial reconstitution that unfolds in "Even an Android Can Cry" be-

tween Vision, his evil robotic creator Ultron, and Ultron's emotionally trou-
bled superheroic creator Goliath illustrates in spectacular fashion how adapt-
ing soap opera to superhero comics meant attaching melodrama's semantic
elements directly to superheroic persona themselves. When Hank Pym suffers a dissociative episode, he develops an entirely new superhero identity—
Yellowjacket—who then "murders" his previous superhero identity, Goliath.
Similarly, when Pym creates a murderous robot "son," he fights for his life
thinking, "It's . . . unbelieveable! In seconds that robot's called me everything from da-da to father [. . .] and now it wants to kill its imagined parent!
It's like a living, mechanized Oedipus Complex" (Thomas and Buscema
1968, 14). No longer were fight scenes primarily about foiling the supervillain's criminal schemes. Superheroes now routinely clashed with superpow-
ered family members and worked out their private psychodrama by brawling,
allegorically, in the streets. In their histrionic suffering, grief, and fisticuffs,
Spider-Man, The Thing, The Hulk, Captain America, the Silver Surfer, and
Vision, among so many others, shrugged off hegemonic masculinity's taboo
on male tears, demonstrating over and over that masculinity and vulnerability
need not be mutually exclusive.

At the same time, in some ways, the emergence of masculine melodrama
at Marvel seemed more like a compromise than a gender revolution. The
particular ways in which these stories integrated the "pathetic" dimensions of
subjectivity formerly excluded by hegemonic masculinity hints at a corporate
sensibility geared toward managing the "gender trouble" created by Marvel's
appropriation of feminine genres like romance comics and daytime soap
operas for a mass audience of young, presumptively heterosexual male readers. In other words, Marvel's reimagining of the ostensibly powerful male
superhero as a "feminized" sufferer not only in private, but in the full expressivity of his superheroic identity, involved not just a "feminizing" of the male
hero, but a reciprocal "masculinizing" of the feminine genre of soap opera.
While comics creators clearly valued the vitalizing effect of popular serial
melodrama as a means of hooking more sophisticated readers, whose own
private struggles in an era of gender trouble for normative masculinity made
an identification with emotionally vulnerable "heroes with problems" appealing, they were also careful not to stray too far from the masculine ego-fantasy
that drew this audience in the first place. Thus, on the one hand, Marvel's
weeping heroes registered uncertainty about midcentury gender norms and
melodramatic superhero-supervillain confrontations allegorized these anxieties. On the other hand, the conventional satisfactions of action and superheroics were still deployed to manage the representation of male "weakness."
Unsurprisingly, costumed spectacle was still accorded narrative precedence
over sequences featuring the hero's fragile male alter ego, indicating the
degree to which "feminine" feeling still had to be subordinated to "masculine" action. In other words, the general rule of hegemonic gender comport-

ment for male superheroes still applied: even though "mainstream [male] superheroes are allowed to express strong agency in public spheres, such as exploring broad political and societal themes[. . . they] are [still] locked into tight boxes when exploring private spheres of what it means to be male" (Voelker-Morris and Voelker-Morris 2014, 102). Given masculine melodrama's self-imposed limitations at Marvel, it is not surprising that the publisher's strategic modulation of phallic masculinity in comics of the 1960s and 1970s began losing ground to more reactionary developments in American culture at large.

SENTIMENTALITY AND THE
NEW SUPERHERO MELODRAMA

The degree to which Wolfman and Pérez's 1984 *The New Teen Titans* constituted a break with genre conventions around superhero melodrama was in many ways implicit in the corporate reshuffling from which the project was born. Wolfman had been writing for Marvel Comics since 1972, served as editor in chief of its black and white publications from 1974 to 1975, and then as editor in chief for the company from 1975 to 1976. Ultimately, however, this relationship soured when a dispute over creative control of *Tomb of Dracula* culminated in Wolfman's defection to industry rival DC Comics in 1980. At the invitation of fellow ex-Marvel alumnus and friend Len Wein, who was already an editor at DC, Wolfman set out to revive the widely scorned *Teen Titans* property that had run sporadically from 1966–1978 (Tucker 2017, 113–14). The original *Teen Titans* series consisted of teen sidekicks of better-known DC heroes like Batman, Wonder Woman, Flash, Aquaman, and Green Arrow. Working closely with former Marvel artist Pérez, Wolfman reinvented the team, retaining some of the original Teen Titans—Robin (Dick Grayson), Wonder Girl (Donna Troy), and Kid Flash (Wally West)—as well as adding a number of new characters: orange-skinned alien princess, Starfire (Koriand'r); African American cybernetic hero, Cyborg (Victor Stone); supernatural healer/half-demon, Raven; and green-skinned shapechanger Beast Boy (Garfield Logan, now renamed, Changeling).

As the new team lineup indicated, Wolfman and Pérez saw their series as a strategic break with DC's past. In an editorial entitled "Second Chances," Wolfman identified his and Pérez's approach to superheroes with the creative mantra "Involvement. Care. Love" (Wolfman 1980). Such were the principles informing his intention to tell more psychologically realistic stories in which "characters personalities [. . .] guide the stories" rather than having "stories fit helter-skelter with our heroes" (Wolfman 1980). The revisionist calculus Wolfman outlines in this editorial epitomized the corporate ethos of the mainstream pulp rebellion at DC (Tucker 2017, 157). It also differentiated *The New Teen Titans* from similar books at Marvel. In the face of routine accusations that he was trying to rip-off the success of Claremont's best-selling superhero melodrama *Uncanny X-Men*, Wolfman was defiant. "There is no similarity I can see between [*The New Teen Titans* and *Uncanny X-Men*]," Wolfman stated categorically in 1981. "The characters are totally different, the types of stories Chris likes to write and I like to write are totally different" (Wolfman 1981). Tellingly, his promise "to make the all new *Teen Titans* the greatest comic mag ever" alluded to the tag line of Marvel's first superhero series, the *Fantastic Four*, which famously billed itself as "The World's Greatest Comic Magazine." This allusion to the series that launched the melodramatic revolution in superhero comics at Marvel in the 1960s thus subtly registered Wolfman's simultaneous identification with that Marvel tradition (he had, indeed, written *Fantastic Four* while at Marvel) and his competitive desire to surpass it.

The cornerstone of Wolfman and Pérez's strategy for developing quality superhero melodrama was a new principle of story and plot construction whereby "characterization overwhelms the action" (Wolfman 1988). Marvel had already begun to explore an expanded role for characterization in its stories through its turn toward the emotional range of soap opera. Yet, as we have seen, "action" remained central to the Marvel method and still predominated over the character development associated with the alter ego's suffering and striving. The most immediate formal consequence of Wolfman and Pérez's tinkering with Marvel's formula was a heightened focus on extended dialogue at the expense of conventional battle sequences. Pérez (1985) praised the telenovela-like *Love and Rockets* and Moore's landmark issue-long "interlude" "Rite of Spring" from *Swamp Thing* #34 (1985), quipping that his fantasy would be to draw a story in which characters simply talked: "*My Dinner with André* in comics" (Pérez 1985). Meanwhile, Wolfman aligned his writing with the character-driven stories of the emergent alternative comics market, citing a 1982 issue of *Cerebus* in which the characters "stood in a room and that was it" (Wolfman 1983a) and praising Paul Chadwick's *Concrete* as "a character story" in which "[t]here are no fight scenes" (Wolfman 1988).

In their first experiment with this kind of storytelling, "A Day in the Lives . . ." from *The New Teen Titans* #8 (1981), costumed adventure is almost totally replaced by the kind of smaller, quieter, more "human" stories about the Titans' parochial days off visiting friends, family, lovers, and each other. In this way, Wolfman's script daringly disarticulated the ordinary human alter ego from the superheroic fantasy upon which the dual-identity superhero is premised. In a series of interlaced vignettes, the Teen Titans' alter egos took center stage: Wonder Girl's alter ego Donna Troy coped with the professional frustration of managing a sexist client during a photo shoot;

alien princess Starfire met Donna's ordinary human fiancé, Terry Long; Wally West put aside his Kid Flash identity to have dinner with his parents; Victor Stone (Cyborg) played a game of softball in the park with children whose more prosaic artificial limbs prompt introspection about his own cybernetic "handicap." By strategically focusing on the quotidian side of the dual-identity trope to the exclusion of conventional action, Wolfman indicated not only his attachment to a more realist middlebrow version of melodrama, but also broadcast his indifference to the idealizing and aggrandizing function of the dual-identity superhero as an ego-fantasy delivery-mechanism for readers.

In this regard, his conceptualization of the Titans' superheroics as simply "their job," recalls the deprivileged status of the public sphere in soap opera melodrama, particularly that of CBS prime-time soap *Dallas* (1978–1991), which was a point of reference for Pérez (Wolfman 1983b). Quoting Charlotte Brundson, Ien Ang (1989) notes that even though "the action of soap opera is not restricted to the familial, or quasi-familial institutions," the feminine-coded zone of familial value "*colonizes* the public masculine sphere, representing it from the point of view of the personal" (59–60). So too, in *New Teen Titans*, does Wolfman's qualitative elevation of characterization and the alter ego over superheroic adventure entail a reduction of the latter to the status of public work. This is possible because pleasure and meaning for the Titans reside in the private sphere, so value is determined not by a public facing identity so much as by the private world of the family and interpersonal relationships. A new interest in chronicling the joys and sorrows of ordinary life characterizes the stories that most prominently differentiate Wolfman and Pérez's *The New Teen Titans* from the spectacle of superheroic fantasy.

Supporting and deepening Wolfman's emphasis on characterization in this landmark issue, was the maturation of Pérez's art style. "They each have individual faces," Pérez (1982a) notes about even his earliest graphic depictions of the Titans. "[E]ven without the masks, and even if I were to remove the hairlines, you can tell they're seven individual faces"—an effect he achieved in part by modeling each character on one or more celebrity's face (Pérez 1982a). But Pérez's physical individuation of the Titans was not limited to facial morphology. "[At Marvel] I was considered a 'power' artist," Pérez observes, but for *The New Teen Titans* "I started [. . .] developing a subtlety in my approach to a story that was not there before. [. . . I] tried not to have the characters look so posed" (Pérez 1982a). This new attunement to figural naturalism in which body postures were "more relaxed" differentiated Pérez's *Titans* work from his "slam-bang action" "Marvel style" of the previous decade, contributing an individuating humanism to Wolfman's emphasis on psychologically realistic characterization and the everyday (Pérez 1982a).

A similarly humanistic aesthetic is evident in Wolfman and Pérez's rejection of melodramatic clichés around superhero origin stories. About Wonder Girl, Pérez (1984) states, "We were determined, that she was going to have a background of normalcy [. . . and] not be the daughter of some villain." The wedding of Donna Troy (Wonder Girl) and Terry Long in the special double-sized "Anniversary" issue #50 (1985) of the series was in many ways the culmination of this revisionist superhero aesthetic. Pérez's newfound visual subtlety was given free reign in an extra-length story that broke decisively with the logic of superhero melodrama. The much earlier and generically more typical superhero wedding of Yellowjacket and The Wasp in *Avengers* #60 (1969) was interrupted by a brawl with the Circus of Crime and the revelation that the groom was in fact Janet's believed-to-be-dead former flame Hank Pym (Goliath). By comparison, Donna's relatively uneventful wedding to Terry was clearly melodrama of a different stripe. The only very minor capitulation this issue made to superhero fantasy was a muted, sentimental scene in which Amazon Queen Hippolyta makes a cameo via magic portal from Paradise Island to congratulate Donna and her betrothed. Most notably for Pérez (1985), "none of the characters appear in costume on the cover. . . . It is just a straight wedding picture."

More broadly, Donna's relationship with Terry functioned throughout the series as a touchstone for Wolfman and Pérez's more down-to-earth treatment of superhero melodrama. Although superhero-civilian romantic pairings were staples of the genre (Superman and Lois Lane or the *Fantastic Four*'s Thing and Alicia Masters, for example), Wolfman self-consciously envisioned the Wonder Girl-Terry Long pairing as breaking with the competing superhero melodrama convention of integrating romantic entanglements with superhero adventure in the manner of the Wasp-Yellowjacket wedding. "She's marrying somebody outside the team, who's not a superhero," Wolfman (1983b) observed about Wonder Girl, agreeing with his interviewer that "[t]hat's probably a first." "[Terry] will never be a superhero," nor will there "be a big fight at the wedding" (Wolfman 1983b). The gender-reversal inherent in the Wonder Girl/Terry Long pairing, which led one interviewer to characterize Terry as "Lois Lane as a man," also tellingly aligned Wolfman and Pérez's new emphasis on ordinary human identity over superheroic fantasy with a subversion of "comic book masculinity."

The turn toward a more sentimental interpretation of melodrama likewise played an important role in disrupting conventional images of superhero masculinity. Where sentimentality is concerned, the driving creative force within the partnership was clearly Pérez, whose profound role in shaping the plot and general sensibility of the series led to him being credited as cocreator or coplotter for many stories. Although Wolfman (1983b) often likened the plotting of his lengthy intersecting story arcs in *The New Teen Titans* to writing "a soap opera," Pérez drew a strong distinction between soap opera and popular romance. Whereas soap opera's thematic emphasis on suffering and open-ended serial form results in what Ang (1985) famously calls its "tragic structure of feeling," popular romance is tonally governed by the predictably reassuring "happy ending" for which Harlequin Romances are famed (70–78). "I love to draw happy people," Pérez (1985) acknowledged, adding: "I stopped watching soap operas [. . . because] I couldn't stand the depression all the time. No one ever seemed to be happy" (Pérez 1985). As Pérez would go on to confess, "There's a certain school of comics that seems to deal with exclusively anguish[. . . . I would] love to [draw a romance book]! In a way, both 'Who Is Donna Troy?' and the wedding issue was my statement showing what potential is still there on the great non-superhero romance stuff" (Pérez 1985). "Who Is Donna Troy?," for instance, scrupulously avoided a tragic resolution, despite a tumultuous plot in which Donna discovers that she was purchased as a baby in a black-market adoption following her birth-mother's death from cancer. Wolfman and Pérez carefully balanced these revelations with a surprise eleventh-hour reunion between Donna and her mistakenly presumed-dead adoptive mother. The tear-jerking final page of the main story—in which Donna stands at her birth-mother's grave, speaking in monologue to the dead mother about her newly consolidated sense of identity as daughter, wife, and member of the Titans—is the quintessence of Wolfman-Pérezian sentimental melodrama. Standing at Donna's side, offering her the childhood doll he has repaired, Dick Grayson embodies its new masculine ideal.

Pérez's dislike of soap opera's "tragic structure of feeling" and his interest in nonsuperhero genres helped distinguish *The New Teen Titans* from more relentlessly "depressing" superhero melodramas like *Uncanny X-Men*. Like superheroics, tragedy provided Marvel melodrama with a buffer against potentially negative reader responses to "soap operatic" male vulnerability and feeling. At Marvel, male tears seemed acceptable to male readers so long as they were shed in the name of suffering or grief. Wolfman and Pérez's *The New Teen Titans*, by contrast, was not only a more "realistic" melodrama, in the sense that it focused more consistently on the out-of-costume lives of its heroes; it was also a sentimental melodrama in which happy affects, quiet scenes of satisfied contemplation, laughter, tears of joy, and more-stable-than-usual happy endings featured prominently as a reliable counterweight to melodrama's constant churn. This tonal environment created new opportunities for vulnerability and emotional expressivity among all the characters. For the male Titans in particular, though, this affective environment was transformative since it broke with the superhero genre's usual redirection of male emotional excess into sublimating violence. Within this context, Pérez's affection for drawing dewy-eyed men who smile acquired a surprisingly subversive charge.

In many ways, the addition of a new Titans character, Jericho (Joseph Wilson), in 1984, crowned the series' convergent investments in quality, sentimentality, and a gentler, more loving masculine ideal. A mute visual artist with the power to temporarily "possess" another person's body by making eye contact with them, Jericho was characteristically depicted as the most sensitive male Titan:

> [Joseph is] a listener, since he can't talk. [. . .] He likes people. Joseph has the soul of an artist—warm, loving, caring. He does not harbor grudges, nor is he someone who enjoys the concept of fighting (though he will when he has to). He's someone who's inspired by a loving soul more than by anything else. He paints, is a musician, is into the Arts. He's very bright, and not at all naive. He knows what's going on; he's just a person who very much believes that there can be good in people, sees good where there is, and does not necessarily hate people because they are not good. He knows the score, he just chooses to walk by himself in many ways, though he is with the Titans. (Wolfman 1984)

In addition to embodying the qualities of counterhegemonic masculinity the series idealized, Jericho's muteness amplified his expressive capacity insofar as it presented Pérez with the artistic challenge of communicating male emotion through his rendering of nuanced, realistic facial expressions. The extraordinary effect of this practice was the production of a comprehensive visual archive of masculine feeling.

Because he is a sentimental visual artist, Jericho reads as a metafictional self-portrait of Pérez. I want to suggest, however, that he might even more accurately be appreciated as a condensed figure for the Wolfman-Pérez collaboration as a whole since the warm professional relationship between the series' creators dramatized the very mode of alternative masculinity Jericho embodied. Such a convergence between series ethos and creative practice was evident in the numerous interviews conducted by the comics industry. Frequently describing their collaboration as a dialectical "give-and-take," Pérez would lay out and illustrate the plot based on Wolfman's story notes, sometimes adding his own scenes and annotating his artwork, which Wolfman would then script. "Marv and I live about half a mile from each other, so it's a very close relationship in the way we work," Pérez noted in 1982. "As far as any of the books I've done, it is probably the most unified effort I've ever worked on." "The book suffers from absolutely no ego problems." "It's incredible. I've never worked on a book where I've had so much feeling that it is a work of love that everyone enjoys" (Pérez 1982a). Wolfman concurred: "I've known George, liked George, and since become a friend of George's. [. . .] So I just find working with him an absolute dream" (Wolfman 1983b). The warm professional friendship and creative process that come into view in interviews of the period suggests that the counterhegemonic masculinity celebrated in *The New Teen Titans* owes no small part of its presentation to the model of homosocial artistic practice embodied by the series' cocreators.

THE NEW TEEN TITANS, QUEER PEDAGOGIES

The formal and tonal revisions to superhero melodrama have had real consequences for the depiction of superhero masculinity, especially for young queer readers. Wolfman's commitment to characterization over action, his heightened disarticulation of the alter ego from the dual identity superhero, and his indifference to the power fantasy usually supported by the latter led him to present all the Titans, regardless of gender, as sensitive, emotionally complex, and thoughtful young people animated by the idealization of an ethical, loving, and (in most cases) temperamentally nonviolent sociability. As Pérez observed (2002), Wolfman "wanted to make [*New Teen Titans*] a super-group [in something] that wasn't quite a superhero book," and this was particularly apparent in his desire "to get those best elements that made books like *Fantastic Four* successful—that sense of family and camaraderie." Pérez's identification of *Fantastic Four* as the most plausible Marvel model for Wolfman's revisionist approach to melodrama was telling. Among Marvel's earliest superhero offerings, *Fantastic Four* was unique in its rejection of the secret identity trope that Wolfman and Pérez's characters would similarly mostly ignore. Even more significantly, as Fawaz (2016) has argued, *Fantastic Four* was, in a sense, already reimagining the heteronormative family of the Eisenhower era along "mutant" lines that made it particularly attractive to queer appropriation (66–93).

With respect to the representation of superhero masculinities, Pérez's understanding of *The New Teen Titans* as a new take on Marvel's already queered "first family" was prophetic. It anticipated the sporadic queer masculinities that cropped up in superhero comics of the late 1980s and early 1990s in counterpoint to that era's dominant mode of reactionary male fantasy. Grant Morrison's "already queered" *Flex Mentallo* (Landon 2007, 201), for instance, or Alan Moore's *Swamp Thing* (Johnson 2011; McDonald and Vena 2016), or the "new Black superhero[es]" of Milestone Media (Brown 1999, 26). Wolfman and Pérez's *The New Teen Titans* offered readers of the previous decade "an alternative to the extreme of hypermasculinity" by presenting male heroes whose virtue was focally identified with emotional vulnerability and more realistic bodily images and postures that made room for traditionally nonmasculine values of softness, gentleness, and humor (Brown 1999, 26–28). Through the youngest, physically smallest, and most flagrantly slapstick Titan's endless teenaged sexual posturing, Wolfman comically cut the egotism of phallic masculinity down to size. In Changeling's odd-couple friendship with sensitive "ghetto youth" Victor Stone (Cyborg), Wolfman critically complicated the pleasures of liberal homosociality while making Cyborg a role model for Changeling, presenting a transvalued black "subordinate masculinity" (Brown 1999, 28). In Dick Grayson's platonic friendship with Donna Troy and Victor Stone's parallel friendship with Sarah Simms, Wolfman provided models of heterosexual male-female relationships based on empathy, trust, love, and mutual respect rather than professional partnership, romance, or the promise of sexual enjoyment. In the revisionist ambience of Wolfman and Pérez's young adult soap opera, the concertedly thematized disruption of normative scripts of gender and (hetero)sexuality were "queer" in the sense that Michael Warner (1993) means when he writes that "'queer'—a term initially generated in the context of terror—has the effect of pointing out a wide field of normalization, rather than simple intolerance, as the site of violence" (xxvi).

For gender nonconforming protogay male readers, the sentimental masculinities of Robin, Cyborg, Changeling, Kid Flash, and Jericho were undoubtedly appealing as sites of projection and recognition, despite the characters' explicitly marked heterosexuality. Pérez's art—whose exactingly detailed style has aptly been called "masturbatory"—played a significant role in facilitating such projections, given as it was to highlight the male body as a site of optical pleasure (Pérez 1982b). "I'm very big on the sexual appeal of my characters—particularly males," Pérez (1987) confirms. As he notes about his "very virile Robin," "Marv was being complimented on his characterization; I was being complimented on making Robin look like an adult at last" (Pérez 1984). Significantly, Robin's virility was being celebrated in a context that was highly conscious of the character's queer associations. "Since Dick Grayson has been established as being 19, and Batman has been established as 29," said Pérez in 1984, "suddenly the man-boy relationships between men 29 and 19 did not work; they were two men." If *Titans* officially disavowed a queer reading of the adult Robin by pairing him romantically with alien warrior-sexpot Starfire, the series nonetheless retained and even flaunted Robin's availability to fandom's erotic gaze. About his visual inclusion of real life members of the Teen Titans Fan Club in some scenes in the Donna Troy wedding issue, for instance, Pérez (1985) notes: "the four women who were ogling Dick and Bruce are four women who are very big Robin fans. [. . . A]ll of them I've talked to, and I know what their views are about Dick Grayson, so I had to do that little scene in the kitchen." Making Robin the sexual object of a female gaze did not, of course, preclude his availability as a homoerotic object for queer male readers—indeed, it licensed it.

If *The New Teen Titans* created an imaginative space in which queer male readers could both recognize themselves and erotically objectify psychologically complex, physically idealized, emotionally nurturing male superhero figures—as it did for me—the play of queer projection and recognition it enabled did not limit itself to the male Titans alone. The commonplace dynamic of cross-gender identification among gay male comics fans meant that queer male fans might equally recognize themselves in Wonder Girl, Starfire, and Raven (Spieldenner 2013, 236–37). Indeed, the privileged status of Donna Troy as a queer icon for gay comics fans is likely traceable to the character's sentimental depiction and deep emotional bonding with Robin in "Who Is Donna Troy?" The story's special status as an exemplar of "quality" popular art, was a further marker of suggestive difference. Similar arguments might be advanced about statuesque, sexually liberated, orange-skinned alien princess Starfire's iconographic compatibility with drag culture, or the queer (nonnormative) resonances of mystic/empath Raven's paranoia that her perverse and sexually potent father Trigon will demonically "possess" her. Ultimately, male and female Titans were available as sites for the projection of queer affects and recognitions, regardless of their gender because the queerness of *The New Teen Titans* inhered not simply in the graphic delineation of alternative masculinities, but in the way Wolfman and Pérez's revision of superhero melodrama so thoroughly problematized traditional gender and genre distinctions. Through techniques of heightened realism and naturalism, the strategic sidelining of superhero action and costumed spectacle in favor of dialogue, and the affective leavening of melodrama's "tragic structure of feeling" with sentimentality, Wolfman and Pérez restored and even amplified the "feminine" soap opera elements that the Marvel superhero melodrama had carefully occluded with capes and fight scenes.

My discussion of the implications of this radically affirmative aesthetic of sentimental masculine melodrama for gender nonconforming, queer or protoqueer boys has been strategic, not exhaustive. It would of course be desirable to explore the sexual and gender implications of comics like Wolfman and Pérez's *The New Teen Titans* for female and trans readers. Instead I have focused on gender nonconforming and protoqueer male readers in part because those terms describe my own standpoint in 1983, and my methodological position is one that sees fan-scholar autoethnography as a vital resource for the recovery and analysis of histories of queer affect. Without it, the reparative importance of such reading strategies and lifeworlds would remain unrecorded and untheorized. I have also focused on the implications of representations of counterhegemonic masculinities in superhero comics for such readers because, despite the evident presence of female readers, boys and young men remained the presumptive primary audience of superhero comics throughout the 1970s and 1980s. Within this context, the disruption of hegemonic gender norms and (gendered) genre associations was tacitly addressed to that young male audience. For boys who comfortably identified with the hegemonic norms of masculinity, *The New Teen Titans'* subtle queering of masculine melodrama presented a dialogic and potentially enlarging alternative to the more reactionary versions of male fantasy already being celebrated in Hollywood. For boys who experienced their gender and/or sexuality as anomalous in the early 1980s, *The New Teen Titans* provided one particularly magnetic site of psychically affirming recognition and imaginative nurture. To me, at age eleven, the concatenation of these circumstances suggested the existence of an adult world that even the anomalous might find habitable.

In her historic 1993 essay, "How to Bring Your Kids up Gay: The War on Effeminate Boys," Sedgwick looks back critically over the institutional homophobia and "effeminophobia" in psychoanalytic and psychiatric discourses of the gay child in the 1980s. She also turns her gaze to the elision of the effeminate boy within queer theory itself. Although she recognizes the political expediency of the gay movement's interruption of "a long tradition of viewing gender and sexuality as continuous and collapsible categories," she nonetheless worries about queer theory's "relative de-emphasis of the links between gay adults and gender-nonconforming children" (Sedgwick 1993, 157). The danger posed by queer theory's early focus on disarticulating gender-nonconformity from sexual object-choice is that it "may leave the effeminate boy once more in the position of the haunting abject—this time the haunting abject of gay thought itself" (Sedgwick 1993, 157). This prospect is especially alarming in light of research confirming that

> for any given adult gay man, wherever he may be at present on a scale of self-perceived or socially ascribed masculinity [. . .] the likelihood is disproportionately high that he will have a childhood history of self-perceived effeminacy, femininity, or nonmasculinity. In this case the eclipse of the effeminate boy from gay adult discourse would represent more than a damaging theoretical gap; it would represent a node of annihilating homophobic, gynephobic, and pedophobic hatred internalized and made central to gay-affirmative analysis. The effeminate boy would come to function as the discrediting open secret of many politicized adult gay men. (Sedgwick 1993, 157–58)

Without intending to, perhaps, *The New Teen Titans* created a zone of affective safety in the "war" on gender-nonconforming boys and future gay men that Sedgwick describes. It made differently nuanced masculinities visible and thus thinkable. In this sense, it was a popular form of queer pedagogy. Its "method" of instruction was rooted in the affective pleasure and moral polarization that are sentimental melodrama's principal domains. Its impacts, like the impacts of all our most intimate texts, are difficult to ascertain and even harder to generalize about. But for those of us who shared in them, and who survived homophobia's and gynophobia's internalized and self-directed aggressions, they are undeniable.

REFERENCES

Ang, Ien. 1985. *Watching Dallas: Soap Opera and the Melodramatic Imagination*. Translated by Della Kouling. New York: Routledge.

Bainbridge, Jason. 2009. "'Worlds within Worlds': The Role of Superheroes in the Marvel and DC Universes." In *The Contemporary Comic Book Superhero*, edited by Angela Ndalianis, 64–85. New York: Routledge.

Brooks, Peter. 1995. *The Melodramatic Imagination: Balzac, Henry James, Melodrama, and the Mode of Excess*. New Haven: Yale University Press.

Brown, Jeffrey A. 1999. "Comic Book Masculinity and the New Black Superhero." *African American Review* 33(1): 25–42.

Bukatman, Scott. 2003. *Matters of Gravity: Special Effects and Supermen in the 20th Century*. Durham, NC: Duke University Press.

Easton, Lee. 2010. "No Endings? No Problem! Reboot, Rinse, Repeat." In *Secret Identity Reader: Essays on Sex, Death, and the Superhero*, edited by Lee Easton and Richard Harrison, 237–51. Hamilton, ON: Wolsak & Wynn.

Fawaz, Ramzi. 2016. *The New Mutants: Superheroes and the Radical Imagination of American Comics*. New York: New York University Press.

Jeffords, Susan. 1994. *Hard Bodies: Hollywood Masculinity in the Reagan Era*. New Brunswick, NJ: Rutgers University Press.

Johnson, Brian. 2011. "Libidinal Ecologies: Eroticism and Environmentalism in Alan Moore's *Swamp Thing*." In *Sexual Ideology in the Works of Alan Moore: Critical Essays on the Graphic Novels*, edited by Todd A. Comer and Joseph M. Sommers, 16–27. Jefferson, NC: McFarland.

Klein, Alan M. 1993. *Little Big Men: Bodybuilding Subculture and Gender Construction*. Albany: SUNY Press.

Klock, Geoff. 2006. *How to Read Superhero Comics and Why*. New York: Continuum.

Landon, Richard. 2007. "A Half-Naked Muscleman in Trunks: Charles Atlas, Superheroes, and Comic Book Masculinity." *Journal of the Fantastic in the Arts* 18(2): 200–16.

Lopes, Paul. 2009. *Demanding Respect: The Evolution of the American Comic Book*. Philadelphia: Temple University Press.

McDonald, Robin Alex, and Dan Vena. 2016. "Monstrous Relationalities: The Horrors of Queer Eroticism and 'Thingness' in Alan Moore and Stephen Bissette's *Swamp Thing*." In *Plant Horror: Approaches to the Monstrous Vegetal in Fiction and Film*, edited by Dawn Keetley and Angela Tenga, 197–214. London: Palgrave Macmillan.

Nelson, Tim. 2004. "Even an Android Can Cry." *Journal of Gender Studies* 13(3): 251–57.

Pérez, George. 1982a. Interview by Richard Howell. *Comics Feature* 19. *New Teen Titans*: Archives (1980–1990). *Titans Tower*. Accessed February 7, 2019. http://www.titanstower.com/comics-feature-19-its-an-interview-with-george-perez/.

———. 1982b. Interviewed by Lone Star Comics. *New Issue Club Express* 117. *New Teen Titans*: Archives (1980–1990). *Titans Tower*. Accessed February 7, 2019. http://www.titanstower.com/new-issue-club-express-117-the-titans-speak/.

———. 1984. "Subtlety and Power: The George Pérez Interview." Interview by Michael F. Hopkins. *New Teen Titans*: Archives (1980–1990). *Titans Tower*. Accessed February 7, 2019. http://www.titanstower.com/amazing-heroes-50-1984/.

———. 1985. Interview by Heidi MacDonald. *Focus on George Perez*. *New Teen Titans*: Archives (1980–1990). *Titans Tower*. Accessed February 7, 2019. http://www.titanstower.com/focus-on-george-perez/.

———. 1987. Interview by Andy Mangels. *Comics Interview* 50. *New Teen Titans*: Archives (1980–1990). *Titans Tower*. Accessed February 7, 2019. http://www.titanstower.com/comics-interview-50-an-interview-with-george-perez/.

———. 2002. Interview by Bill Baker. *Comic Book Marketplace* 89. *New Teen Titans*: Archives (1980–1990). *Titans Tower*. Accessed February 7, 2019. http://www.titanstower.com/the-best-of-all-worlds-george-perez/.

Pizzino, Christopher. 2016. *Arresting Development: Comics at the Boundaries of Literature*. Austin: University of Texas Press.

Sedgwick, Eve Kosofsky, and Adam Frank. 2003. *Touching Feeling: Affect, Pedagogy, Performativity. Durham*: Duke University Press.

Sedgwick, Eve Kosofsky. 1993. "How to Bring Your Kids up Gay: The War on Effeminate Boys." In *Tendencies*, edited by Eve Kosofsky Sedgwick, 154–64. Durham, NC: Duke University Press.

Spieldenner, Andrew R. 2013. "Altered Egos: Gay Men Reading across Gender Difference in *Wonder Woman*." *Journal of Graphic Novels and Comics* 4(2): 235–44.

Thomas, Roy, and John Buscema. 1968. "Even an Android Can Cry!" *Avengers* 1(57). New York: Marvel Comics.

———. 1969. ". . . Till Death Do Us Part!" *Avengers* 1(60). New York: Marvel Comics.

Tucker, Reed. 2017. *Slugfest: Inside the Epic 50-Year Battle between Marvel and DC*. London: Sphere.

Voelker-Morris, Robert, and Julie Voelker-Morris. 2014. "Stuck in Tights: Mainstream Superhero Comics' Habitual Limitations on Social Constructions of Male Superheroes." *Journal of Graphic Novels and Comics* 5(1): 101–17.

Warner, Michael. 1993. Introduction. *Fear of a Queer Planet: Queer Politics and Social Theory*, edited by Michael Warner. vii–xxxi. Minneapolis: University of Minnesota Press.

Wilde, Jenée. 2011. "Queer Matters in *The Dark Knight Returns*: Why We Insist on a Sexual Identity for Batman." *Riddle Me This Batman!: Essays on the Universe of the Dark Knight*, edited by Kevin K. Durand and Mary K. Leigh. 104–23. Jefferson, NC: McFarland.

Wolfman, Marv. 1980. "Second Chances." *The New Teen Titans* 2. New Teen Titans: Archives (1980–1990). *Titans Tower*. Accessed February 7, 2019. http://www.titanstower.com/ntt-2-second-chances/.

———. 1981. Interview by Mark Shainblum. *Orion* 2. New Teen Titans: Archives (1980–1990). *Titans Tower*. Accessed February 7, 2019. http://www.titanstower.com/orion-2-marv-wolfman-interview/.

———. 1983a. Interview by Dwight R. Decker. *The Comics Journal* 79. New Teen Titans: Archives (1980–1990). *Titans Tower*. Accessed February 7, 2019. http://www.titanstower.com/comics-journal-79-marv-wolfman-interview/.

———. 1983b. Interview by Heidi MacDonald. *The Comics Journal* 80. New Teen Titans: Archives (1980–1990). *Titans Tower*. Accessed February 7, 2019. http://www.titanstower.com/comics-journal-80-marv-wolfman-interview/.

———. 1984. "The Titans' Other Half." Interview by Michael F. Hopkins. *Amazing Heroes* 50. New Teen Titans: Archives (1980–1990). *Titans Tower*. Accessed February 7, 2019, http://www.titanstower.com/amazing-heroes-50-1984/.

———. 1988. Interview by Kevin Dooley. *Amazing Heroes* 135. New Teen Titans: Archives (1980–1990). *Titans Tower*. Accessed February 7, 2019. http://www.titanstower.com/amazing-heroes-135-1988-a-marv-wolfman-interview/.

Wolfman, Marv, and George Pérez. 1981. "A Day in the Lives. . . ." *The New Teen Titans* 1(8). New York: DC Comics.

———. 1984. "Who Is Donna Troy?" *The New Teen Titans* 1(38). New York: DC Comics.

———. 1985. "We Are Gathered Here Today. . . ." *Tales of the Teen Titans* 1(50). New York: DC Comics.

Index

About the Editors and Contributors

EDITORS

Sean Parson, Ph.D., is an assistant professor in the departments of Politics and International Affairs and the Master's Program in Sustainable Communities at Northern Arizona University. He is completing a book manuscript on *Food Not Bombs* and urban anarchism, and is also working on a book manuscript on critical animal studies, environmental political theory, and comic studies. He has written on a range of topics from social movement theory and climate justice, to film studies, comic studies, and critical animal studies.

J. L. Schatz, Ph.D., is the director of debate at Binghamton University where he serves as a lecturer and teaches courses on Media & Politics out of the English Department. He has published book chapters on representations of apocalypse in the *Terminator* films, the construction of disability in the *Resident Evil* films, and ecological security in the TV show *Lost*. Dr. Schatz has also published peer reviewed journal articles on apocalypse and the environment as well as subjectivity in relation to teaching pedagogy in debate. Beyond his own publications he has coedited a special issue for the *Journal of Critical Animal Studies*, a book titled *Screening the Nonhuman*, and has been in charge of organizing several conferences, including the thirteeth and fourteenth annual North America Institute for Critical Animal Studies and the first and second annual Eco-Ability Conference.

CONTRIBUTORS

Hailey J. Austin is a comics Ph.D. student at the University of Dundee, Scotland. Her doctoral research focuses on animal comics, anthropomorphism and trauma. As part of her research, she has published a public information comic, *Chronicle: The Archive and Museum Anthology,* with Uni-Verse as well as a comic that was adopted onto the second year film noir module at the University of Dundee titled *The Big Sheep.* Her other research interests include female agency, noir, music in comics, archives, and transmedia. She has previously published a book chapter on transmedia and *The Walking Dead* with IGI Global, an article on intergenerational trauma and *Maus* with *Colloquy* journal, and several interviews and book reviews in *Studies in Comics*. Her article on music and noir in *Blacksad* is forthcoming this year in the open access journal, *ComicsGrid*. She is also a published comics writer, having written scripts for DC Thomson's *Commando* comics.

Julian Barr is a Ph.D. candidate in Geography at the University of Washington Seattle. He has a BA in history and a MS in geography both from the St. Louis area. He is interested in queer-feminist geography, qualitative methodology, and cultural geography with a focus on place studies and popular culture. His research is focused on the historical geography of lesbian and queer women in Seattle with a focus on place/community development. His secondary research interests include researching issues of representation of identity and place in popular culture.

Anne Bialowas, Ph.D., is an associate professor in the Department of Communication at Weber State University. She teaches undergraduate courses in communication theory, media studies, and gender in addition to graduate courses in advanced presentations, team-building, and facilitation. Her research interests encompass sport communication, rhetoric, and gender studies.

T. J. Buttgereit is a Ph.D. student in Philosophy at Binghamton University with undergraduate degrees in Philosophy, Politics, and Law and History. His academic interests center around Disability Studies in which he has written numerous essays within a variety of disciplines. He debated on the national level for the Binghamton Speech and Debate Team, where he met Emily Mendelson.

Ryan Cheek, is the assistant director of Forensics and an instructor in the Department of Communication at Weber State University where he received his MA. He teaches undergraduate courses in communication theory, communication law, interpersonal and small group communication, and argumentation studies in addition to coaching a nationally competitive collegiate policy debate program. His research interests encompass political rhetoric, masculinity, and argumentation studies.

Kevin Cummings, Ph.D., is professor and chair of the Department of Communication Studies and Theatre at Mercer University, and he is an affiliated faculty member in the Department of Women and Gender Studies. His research explores the intersections between rhetoric and media, including scholarship on artificial intelligence, invasive species, and Twitter. His publications include essays in *Controversia*, *Critical Problems in Argumentation*, *The Handbook of Media and Mass Communication Theory*, and a chapter in the book *Communication and Control*. With James Stanescu, he coedited *The Ethics and Rhetoric of Invasion Ecology*.

Kiera Gaswint graduated from Bowling Green State University with her Master's degree in Literary and Textual Studies in May 2018. During her time at BGSU, Kiera was an active participant in the introductory writing program and a fiction editor at BGSU's creative graduate journal, the *Mid-American Review*. Kiera's research activities include gender representations in popular media, such as comics, film, and television. Her recent publications include her thesis, "A Comparative Study of Women's Aggression."

Brian Johnson, Ph.D., is an associate professor of English and Women's and Gender Studies at Carleton University in Ottawa, Ontario. Recently, his articles on H. P. Lovecraft's philosophy, influences, and sexuality have appeared in *The Age of Lovecraft* (Minnesota, 2016), *The Lovecraftian Poe* (Lehigh 2017), and *New Directions in Supernatural Horror Literature* (Palgrave 2018). His current research explores intersections between superhero comics, melodrama, and queer feeling.

Emily Mendelson is a senior at Binghamton University studying business analytics and women, gender, and sexuality studies. She researches the intersection of college hookups, consent, and disability studies, and is also conducting data visualization research focusing on color theory and cognition. Emily met her coauthors from her time on the Binghamton Speech and Debate Team, and extremely grateful to have had the opportunity to publish with them.

Jacob Murel is a Ph.D. student at Northeastern University in Boston, MA, where he studies visual culture and methods of digital image analysis. He has published and presented several papers on film and literature and is a regularly contributing reviewer to *The Comics Journal*.

David J. Roberts, Ph.D., is associate professor, Teaching Stream in the Urban Studies Program at the University of Toronto. His research interests include the geographies of race and racialization, urban infrastructure planning, and the politics of public participation in urban knowledge production and policymaking. He also has a keen interest in how popular culture shapes what we know about cities.

Edgar Sandoval is currently a Ph.D. Candidate at the Department of Geography at the University of Washington Seattle. He graduated with a BA in Geography and Political Science from Dartmouth College. Edgar's doctoral research is on how undocumented migrants navigate their everyday lives in Los Angeles despite violence, with a particular interest in media representations. His secondary research interests relate to the construction of space in relation to difference and power in popular culture.